Long Island

YESTERDAY & TODAY ™

Gary W. Wojtas

WEST
SIDE
PUBLISHING

Gary W. Wojtas is a veteran writer and editor about all things Long Island. His previous book, *Long Island: Reflections on a Miracle*, was published in 2005. Wojtas has written more than 2,000 articles about Long Island and its people and places and he is an award-winning editor and columnist for *Long Island* magazine. He recently completed his doctoral degree in Educational Leadership and Technology at Dowling College and is an adjunct professor, teaching magazine writing and public relations, at Manhattan College. Wojtas lives with his wife and three children on Long Island.

For more than 35 years, **Bruce Bennett** and his company Bruce Bennett Studios (BBS) was a leader in supplying Long Island with its photographic needs. Mostly known for ice hockey photography, Bruce sold BBS to Getty Images in 2004 and joined them as their director of photography, hockey imagery. He lives on Long Island with his wife Betty Ann and two children Melanie and Max. His Web page is www.longislandny.com.

James Robertson has been an avid photographer ever since a college photography course in the mid-1960s. He has traveled extensively, not only in the vicinity of Long Island, but also through the rest of the United States, Western Europe, Australia, and New Zealand. Visit his Web site, www.pbase.com/jimrob for more.

Facts verified by **Hollie Deese**.

Front cover: Greenport, New York

Yesterday & Today is a trademark of Publications International, Ltd.

West Side Publishing is a division of Publications International, Ltd.

Louis Weber, CEO
Publications International, Ltd.
7373 North Cicero Avenue
Lincolnwood, Illinois 60712

Permission is never granted for commercial purposes.

ISBN-13: 978-1-60553-901-0
ISBN-10: 1-60553-901-5

Manufactured in China.

8 7 6 5 4 3 2 1

Library of Congress Control Number: 2010920615

This shell mosaic is one of three located at Old Westbury Gardens. The work was completed in 1969 by Artemis Housewright.

Contents

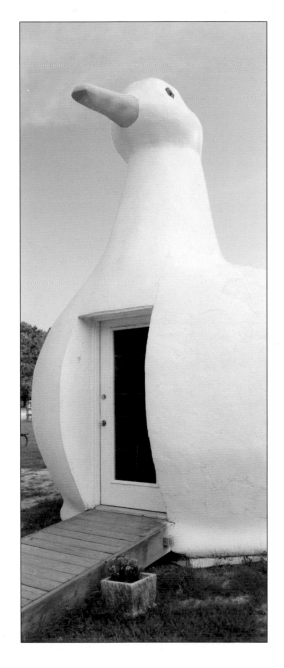

An Island of Plenty, a Land of Firsts

For many suburban communities across the country, tracing history is as easy as looking at incorporation papers and reading a history book. This isn't the case with Long Island. Its complex and diverse origins span cultures of Native Americans, settlers, and fishermen. The founding of Southold, its first community, can be traced all the way back to 1640.

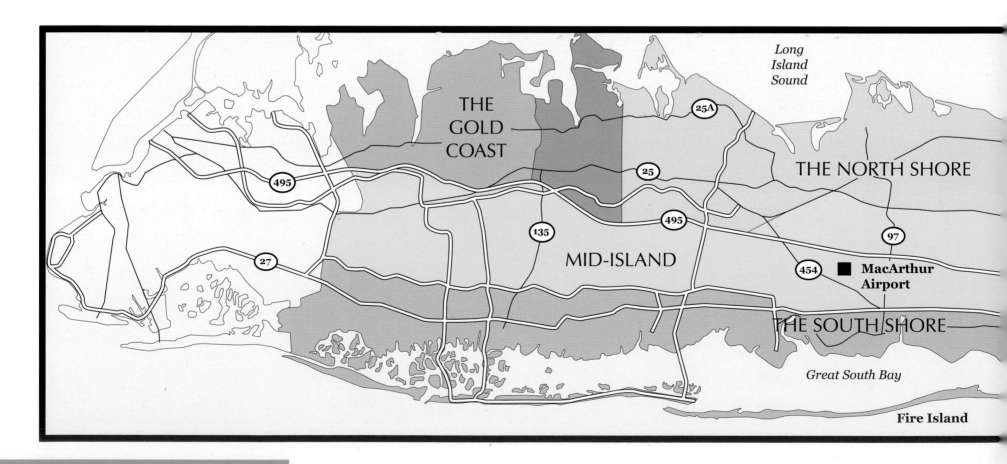

Since then, Long Island's evolution has brought with it many groundbreaking firsts. The first transatlantic flight, the first radio transmission, the first American suburb, and the first man on the moon all had connections to Long Island. The ATM was developed on Long Island, as was *Tennis for Two*, the first video game, which was created at the Brookhaven National Laboratory.

Over the course of its history, Long Island and its residents have played a vital role in many of this country's important events. The Battle of Long Island was an early turning point of the

This plaque is a replica of the one *Apollo 11* astronauts left on the moon in 1969. The *Apollo 11* lunar module was constructed on Long Island at Grumman Aerospace.

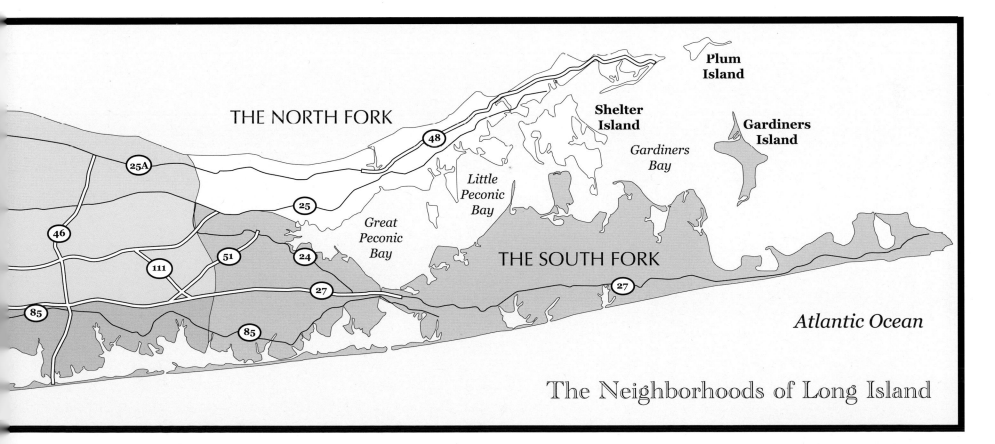

The Neighborhoods of Long Island

Long Island has long been a cradle of technological innovation. In 1932, David Sarnoff (*left*) and Guglielmo Marconi (*right*) visited the RCA tower at Rocky Point—the site of the very first radio transmission.

American Revolution; two sea battles off the coast of Sag Harbor helped the American cause prevail in the War of 1812; and Teddy Roosevelt, probably Long Island's most famous resident, quarantined his Rough Riders along the dunes of the East End after a fierce battle during the Spanish-American War. Several years later, President Roosevelt made influential decisions from the front porch of his "Summer White House," Sagamore Hill in Oyster Bay.

During the 20th century, Long Island was at the core of the aviation boom, which culminated in Lucky Lindy's famous flight from Curtiss Field. That aviation experience was tapped again during World War II. Long Islanders in the defense industry engineered many of the warplanes that helped the American cause in the Great War.

Suburbia was conceptualized and created in Nassau County shortly after World War II. Developer William Levitt transformed the quiet farming community of Island Trees into a haven of residential sprawl for returning GIs and their families. Today, Levittown is one of Long Island's largest communities and still functions as Levitt originally envisioned: a place where people can go to raise a family away from the urban challenges of New York City.

As the space race took off in earnest in the late 1950s, Long Island was at the forefront of another American revolution when, in 1969, Neil Armstrong took his "one small step for man." That famous moon leap came from the lunar module, which was constructed at Grumman Aerospace facilities in Bethpage. After performing the most famous moonwalk in history, the media-shy Armstrong continued his career as an innovator in space technology while working for AIL, a Deer Park–based company.

Today, Long Island has grown and evolved into a diversified community of 2.9 million residents who remain fully entrenched—geographically and oftentimes spiritually—in a world abutting the long shadow of the Big Apple. While Long Islanders still fill city jobs each day in the service, financial, and marketing industries, they remain identified by name and history through their relationship with the sea: the Long Island Sound to the north, the Great South Bay and Atlantic Ocean to the south.

As visitors come to enjoy the beaches, drink the local wine, and play on the world-famous golf courses, and as trendy people of the Hamptons come and go each summer like ocean waves, true Long Islanders enjoy the island for what it continues to provide: a warm, safe, and inviting place to call home.

This idyllic scene at the Montauk Lighthouse is one that is common to Long Island. The region's shorelines are dotted with windmills, lighthouses, and marinas, making it the ideal setting for a peaceful getaway.

In the 1970s, long after the Long Island potato crop had all but dried up, a new industry emerged: wine vinyards. Alex and Louise Hargrave planted the area's very first vineyard in 1973; since then, Long Island has become home to more than 25 wineries. The Pellegrini Vineyard, shown at left, is just one example.

The Gold Coast

The Great Gatsby Meets the Great Estate

The Gold Coast remains Long Island's North Shore region of incredible wealth and opulence. While it reigns supreme today as the choice real estate location on the island, its past is even grander.

At the turn of the 20th century, Long Island was still a rural region of farms and farmers. However, as the horseless carriage became mechanized and the stock market evolved into a viable place to make serious investment dollars, the wealthy captains of Manhattan industry looked to spread their residential wings. The search took them east, away from the opulence of their penthouses and brownstones. This rich man's suburban sprawl whisked the famous and wealthy families of the time—names like Astor, Guggenheim, Woolworth, du Pont, Whitney, and Kahn among them—across the Brooklyn Bridge to Long Island.

The region, spanning from the Queens border to the east and Huntington to the west, caught the attention of these wealthy families because of its natural beauty, available open space, and its proximity to New York City and the Long Island Sound. The rich and famous of the time craved the water views off the cliffs and beaches of Sands Point and Great Neck; they adored the easy access for their sailboats and yachts. At the height of the Gold Coast era (from about 1900 to 1930), hundreds of mansions were constructed in the area.

CAVIAR DREAMS

Grand showplaces were built on huge parcels of land, many numbering more than 50 acres. They included indoor and outdoor pools, ornate statues and wrought iron fencing, arboretum-like planting, and servant quarters. Nothing was off limits. Mansions had hundreds of rooms, gold-plated doorknobs, and golden handrails; the finest wood and

Laurelton Hall in Laurel Hollow, seen here in 1924, was a prime example of Gold Coast extravagance. Built in 1904 by and for Louis Comfort Tiffany, son of Charles Tiffany (Tiffany & Co. founder), the 580-acre estate featured an overlook view of the Long Island Sound. Its interior was an eclectic design of Tiffany glass and art. Unfortunately, the mansion fell into disrepair after its owner's death and was destroyed by a fire in 1957.

Left: While the Gold Coast is now known for its elegance and opulence, the bulk of Long Islanders worked the land during the 19th century. In 1903, a farmer uncovers Long Island's staple crop—the potato—which provided employment, money, and food for the region.

The Lakeville Golf and Country Club, shown in 1927, was a popular retreat for Gold Coast residents. The course hosted the 1932 U.S. Open and is still open today in Great Neck (though renamed the Fresh Meadow Country Club).

metal were shipped from around the world to ensure the builder's vision for the estate was properly met.

Memorialized by F. Scott Fitzgerald in *The Great Gatsby* as East Egg and West Egg (representing Kings Point and Sands Point), the Gold Coast of Long Island was *the* playground for the rich and famous. The parties thrown at the coastal estates of Nassau's North Shore were gatherings of grandeur that attracted kings, queens, barons, and baronesses from Europe and the Far East, trekking in to play with their wealthy peers. The grander the party, the more the party-thrower's reputation grew in the community as a person of real money and taste.

The Gold Coast inhabitants were the poster children for the "Roaring '20s" as they worked hard, earned lots of money, and spent it lavishly on homes, cars, and parties. Polo fields were built, and famous golf course architects were brought to the region to design some of the world's best and most challenging courses.

When the Great Depression struck and the stock market crashed, many of these Gold Coast players quickly lost their fortunes and were forced to either sell their estates at a great loss or simply close them. Without adequate care, these mansions fell into a state of disrepair. Many became ruins over time—destinations for scavenger hunters and curiosity seekers.

However, many of these magnificent estates were converted through the years for more meaningful uses. Otto Kahn's estate, Oheka Castle, has been well kept and currently operates as a swank catering hall and small hotel.

THE NORTH SHORE

The North Shore today benefits from the generosity of some former Gold Coast families who sold, willed, and donated estates for cultural and civic uses. Hillwood, the former Marjorie Merriweather Post estate, was sold in 1951 and was converted into the CW Post Campus of Long Island University. The White Eagle estate of Alfred I. du Pont is now the de Seversky Center on the New York Institute of Technology campus. Other estates became museums and arboretums, like the former Phipps Estate, which is now Old Westbury Gardens, a remarkably well-preserved location to visit and dream of a golden era gone by.

In a literary twist of fate, the Gold Coast once again became world renowned through a novel. In 1997, Long Island's Nelson DeMille penned his best seller titled *The Gold Coast*, a novel focusing on the 21st century lifestyle of a North Shore family.

Today, there are few remaining captains of industry on the North Shore. Nonetheless, the region remains one of the most expensive in Long Island. The land where many of these Gold Coast mansions once stood was sold long ago and subdivided into two-acre lots making way for the *nouveau riche* and their 21st-century "McMansions."

Right: The "Temple of Love" still rests lakeside on the campus of Old Westbury Gardens as a place for couples young and old to visit, view the majestic gardens, and rekindle past love.

F. Scott Fitzgerald (shown here in 1920 with his wife, Zelda, during their honeymoon) modeled the image of affluence he found on Long Island in the early 20th century for his classic novel *The Great Gatsby*. Ironically, Fitzgerald only spent one year of his life living in the area.

THE GREAT GATSBY

In *The Great Gatsby*, the wealthy enclaves of the glamour set were referred to as East and West Egg, but in reality author F. Scott Fitzgerald was describing Long Island's Gold Coast—specifically the communities of Kings Point and Sands Point.

Gatsby is considered by some to be the great American novel; brilliant in its description of American affluence, *Gatsby* captured the arrogance and greed of the newly rich who made money legally in the stock market and illegally as bootleggers.

The term "Jazz Age" was born out of Fitzgerald's novel as a way to characterize the excessive wealth possessed by Gold Coast estate owners. Nick Carraway takes readers inside the lavish parties and peels back the facade of affluence to reveal a cynical, mournful longing at the heart of this seeming American dream.

The Long Island backdrop and connection to *Gatsby* was clear. Fitzgerald lived in Great Neck in 1922 and was able to draw on his experiences to give the book its remarkable authenticity.

The book did not become the best seller Fitzgerald envisioned when it was published in 1925. It was only after Fitzgerald's untimely death in 1940, at the age of 44, that the novel's place as a classic of American literature was recognized and sales skyrocketed. In 1974, Paramount Pictures released a major motion picture based on the novel, starring Robert Redford and Mia Farrow.

Today, *The Great Gatsby* remains required reading; more than 80 years since it was published, *Gatsby* still sells tens of thousands of copies each year.

Robert Redford (as Jay Gatsby) and Mia Farrow (as Daisy Buchanan) starred in the Paramount Pictures version of the classic Fitzgerald novel. The 1974 movie was released to lukewarm reviews. At left, the original novel's dust jacket, printed in 1925, was considered a "haunting" work of art juxtaposing the *Gatsby* glamour with the seedier side of wealth.

NELSON DEMILLE

WHILE GATSBY BROUGHT LIFE to Long Island's Gold Coast, it was a more modern and locally bred author who carried the mantle forward. Nelson DeMille was born in New York City in 1943 but was raised on Long Island in the 1950s and graduated from Elmont High School in 1961. DeMille attended Hofstra University in Hempstead for three years before heading off to Vietnam.

Upon his return, he received his bachelor's degree and began publishing his writing—which was often set in Long Island. His first major novel, *By the Rivers of Babylon*, was released in 1978. While DeMille wrote consistently for the next decade, it was his 1990 blockbuster *The Gold Coast* that made him a superstar writer. The plot revolves around a modern-day Wall Street lawyer—who has an aristocratic past tied to the region's history—and a mafia don, part of the *nouveau riche* who inhabited the 1990s Gold Coast.

OLD WESTBURY GARDENS

Construction on the John S. Phipps estate in Old Westbury began in 1903 and was completed in 1906, opening a remarkable monument to the wealth of the time. Phipps built the home for his wife as a reminder of her family's estate in England. The home is situated on a 200-acre parcel, transforming the area into a pastoral paradise of woodlands, walking trails, ponds, and pools.

Phipps spared no expense in furnishing the 23-room estate by bringing in the finest furnishings and artwork from all over the world. The Phipps family resided in the estate until the mid-1950s when the husband and wife both died.

In 1959, the Phipps children donated the home and gardens to the public. It didn't take long for the grounds to become a favorite site for photo shoots and movie productions. *The Age of Innocence, Wolf, North by Northwest,* and *American Gangster* were all—at least partially—shot at Old Westbury Gardens.

Today, guided tours of the home and gardens are popular with plant lovers, architecture aficionados, and visiting school children. The site hosts many exhibits, lectures, book signings, horticultural demonstrations, and an assortment of workshops.

After three years of construction, the John Phipps estate was completed in 1906. Phipps, heir to the U.S. Steel fortune, spared no expense in building a home that resembled an English manor. He did so on 200 acres in central Nassau County to remind his English wife of home and to honor her heritage. Today, the magnificent estate is the centerpiece of Old Westbury Gardens, one of Long Island's most popular attractions.

The Primrose Path at Old Westbury Gardens is just one of the hundreds of trails and walkways that exist throughout the property. Such flourishes illustrate why Old Westbury is widely considered the finest English garden ever created in the United States.

John Phipps furnished the interior of his manor using the finest furniture from Europe. He designed the walls and ceilings with ornate figurines and carvings. Today, the Phipps home is open to the public and many of the 44 rooms are maintained as they were adorned in 1906.

The Age of Innocence

The beautiful landscaping and ornate architecture of Old Westbury Gardens has always been quite popular with filmmakers looking for scenes of history and affluence. *The Age of Innocence,* starring Daniel Day-Lewis and Michelle Pfeiffer and directed by Martin Scorsese, was filmed extensively on the property in 1992.

The Kings Point campus of the United States Merchant Marine Academy has guarded the New York metropolitan area since its dedication in 1943 by President Franklin Delano Roosevelt. The campus consists of 28 buildings set on 82 acres; approximately 950 midshipmen are housed there.

U.S. MERCHANT MARINE ACADEMY

Prompted by a fire aboard the cruise ship *Morro Castle* in 1934 (in which 137 lives were lost), Congress was convinced that standardized federal maritime training was needed. Subsequently, the Merchant Marine Act of 1936 was passed. Two years later a Merchant Marine Cadet Corps was formed, and on September 30, 1943, President Franklin Delano Roosevelt dedicated the United States Merchant Marine Academy (USMMA) at Kings Point. The Long Island location was chosen for its easy access to the region's waterways.

Through the years the academy continued to be a well-respected institution where leaders in the maritime industry learned basic and advanced shipping methods. During times of war the Merchant Marines become an important "fourth line of defense," delivering weapons and supplies to U.S. troops and

allies. Its students and graduates have served in Korea and Vietnam, and in 1974, the USMMA was the first U.S. service institution to admit women.

The 82-acre campus consists of 28 buildings and houses more than 100 vessels at its waterfront facility. Melville Hall, the campus officers club, was built in 1912 as a summer residence for silent-movie star Thomas Meighan. Its was named after *Moby Dick* author Herman Melville, a former Long Island resident.

Currently, there are about 950 midshipmen at the USMMA. To complete their training, each spend more than a year at sea, traveling the world aboard different types of vessels and learning the shipping industry firsthand.

The Claralea mansion, shown here on a postcard from the early 20th century, still stands at the United States Merchant Marine Academy.

The Webb Institute, another maritime-based school, resides on the former country estate of Herbert L. Pratt. Today, it offers only one academic option, a double major in naval architecture and marine engineering, and is the only private undergraduate program of its kind in the country. The school, which functions under a strict honor code, has only 90 students and boasts a 100 percent job placement rate. Its unique setting and campus also features its own yacht club, English pub, and full automotive workshop.

Merchant Marine Academy graduates are groomed for myriad careers in the military and various shipping industries in this country and abroad. Their rigorous course-work includes more than a year spent at sea.

USMMA graduates have been tossing their hats after every graduation ceremony since 1945.

In keeping with tradition at the United States Merchant Marine Academy, an academy official rings the 1945 Victory Bell during Acceptance Day ceremonies.

FROM MANSION TO COLLEGE

As dictated by the law of entropy, the glitz and glamour of the Roaring '20s eventually dwindled into a prolonged depression. The North Shore's affluence faded, along with the care of its extravagant properties. Refurbishment became the new trend.

In Greenvale, Hillwood was the estate of Marjorie Merriweather Post, sole heir to the Post cereal fortune. Merriweather Post married financier E. F. Hutton, and in 1951 she sold Hillwood to Long Island University for $200,000. In 1954, on the 100th anniversary of Charles Williams Post's birth, C. W. Post College was opened. Today, Hillwood is the centerpiece of the campus that has 8,500 undergraduate students; the building is used as an administrative center and sits on top of a hill adjacent to the campus's great lawn.

Situated next door is the Old Westbury Campus of the New York Institute of Technology (NYIT) and its de Seversky Center. Philanthropist, inventor, and businessman Alfred I. du Pont originally built his estate, White Eagle, on the Gold Coast in 1918 but sold it eight years later. The home was purchased by Frederick and Amy Phipps Guest, who renamed it Templeton. Frederick Guest was a first cousin to Winston Churchill.

The elaborate estate was passed down within the family until 1972 when the NYIT purchased it and renamed it the de Seversky Center after Alexander P. de Seversky, a Russian aviator and NYIT board member. Today, the de Seversky Center serves as a premier special events facility for the region.

Winnick House

Cereal heiress Marjorie Merriweather Post and her second husband, famed financier E. F. Hutton, built this grand Tudor-style home in 1921. It was later sold to Long Island University and is now called Winnick House. Today, it is utilized as an administrative building on the C. W. Post campus.

Alfred I. duPont, a wealthy inventor and businessman, helped shape Long Island's Gold Coast by building his White Eagle estate in 1918. The estate later became part of the New York Institute of Technology.

de Seversky Center

Today, Alfred I. du Pont's mansion serves as an in-demand location for weddings and special occasions. Renamed the de Seversky Center by the NYIT, the grandeur of the estate's past is visible in the elaborate external grounds and through the many original interior furnishings.

POLO

The Meadowbrook Polo Club, located in Old Westbury, was founded in 1881 and prides itself on being the oldest club of its kind in the United States. Its history began as a sportsman's paradise for horse-owning residents on the North Shore of Long Island.

Meadowbrook quickly became the most popular club in the country; from 1923 to 1953 it hosted the prestigious Open Championship. The open and other polo matches regularly drew tens of thousands of spectators who came in droves to see Stephen "Laddie" Sanford, Devereux Milburn, Tommy Hitchcock, Michael Phipps, Stewart Iglehart, and Winston Guest, some of the best known riders of the day.

Author Damon Runyon even waxed poetic about a 1930 Westchester Cup polo match on Long Island: "There was a grand entrance before the game, just like a circus. The ponies were led past the stands, all saddled and bridled, their legs swathed in bandages…" The Long Island Rail Road set up a special stop to bring travelers to the site.

During the early 1900s, polo also made its splash on the fashion scene by developing the button-down collar—so a rider's collar would not flap in his face. And, of course, there's the polo shirt, still a staple of many men's wardrobes.

The original Meadowbrook Polo Club was razed in the name of "progress" when the Meadowbrook Parkway was built through the property in 1954. Today, the club still holds polo matches at its site in Old Westbury and at Bethpage State Park, where the Open Championship returned to Long Island in 1994.

Horse racing, riding, and polo were commonplace along the Gold Coast in the early 1900s. At the Meadowbrook Club, riders clear a water jump during a 1945 steeplechase event.

Mrs. Goodlow McDowell and Mrs. C. Perry Beadleston enjoy the Westbury Cup polo matches held at the Meadowbrook Club in 1929. For the residents of the Gold Coast, this was a typical weekend scene held each summer.

Today, polo remains popular on Long Island. Above, local players compete during a match held at Bethpage State Park. There are several thriving polo clubs that remain active throughout the region.

OHEKA CASTLE

Though small in physical stature, Otto Kahn—banker, financier, and philanthropist—did everything large. On Long Island, his grandest creation was simply (and egotistically) called Oheka Castle, after his own moniker, **O**tto **He**rmann **Ka**hn.

Kahn purchased the 443-acre tract in Cold Spring Harbor in 1914. Its 127 rooms, totaling more than 109,000 square feet, made it the second-largest private residence in the country. When Oheka opened in 1919, its cost was $11 million—yet Kahn utilized Oheka mostly as a summer home, throwing parties for heads of state, celebrities, and business partners.

Its golf course, numerous outbuildings, private airplane landing strip, and working farm added to its charm and allure. Kahn was able to enjoy the property's luster for 15 years until his death in 1934.

In the late 1970s, the castle stood abandoned, a regular target of vandals who set more than 100 fires in five years on the estate's grounds.

After years of neglect, Oheka was down to 23 acres, with much of its original garden splendor removed. Developer Gary Melius purchased the site in 1984 and set out to restore Oheka to its former beauty. Alongside a team of architects and contractors, Melius studied old photos and drawings in an effort to provide as much original detail as possible. The result was a refurbished and once again lavish property, which currently serves as a special events center where visitors can go back in time and remember the glory days of the Gold Coast.

Banker and financier Otto Kahn set out and succeeded in building the region's "Castle." Oheka was his creation, and he utilized more than $11 million of his incredible wealth to open it in 1919.

The 127 rooms of Oheka (photographed circa 1920), were all adorned with the finest furnishings, wall hangings, and floor coverings that money could buy. Only celebrities, clients, prospects, or heads of state were granted invites to Kahn's lavish Oheka bashes.

Oheka has re-emerged as an exclusive catering facility after years of neglect and vandalism robbed the estate's exterior of its original glory. Today, the castle grounds are a popular spot for social events.

COE HALL/ PLANTING FIELDS

Many people trace the beginnings of Long Island's Gold Coast estates to James Beekman, who had what is considered the first architect-designed country home built in the area in the 1860s. From those beginnings sprouted more extravagant estates as Wall Street wealth continued to spread throughout the area.

Coe Hall, built circa 1918 on an estate known as Planting Fields, was one of the most magnificent. Built in the Tudor Revival style and designed by New York–based architects A. Stewart Walker and Leon Gillette, Coe Hall consisted of 65 rooms spread over four floors. The servant's wing alone accommodated 13 staff members; the home included a refrigeration room, wine cellar, valet's apartment, and a floral arranging room.

At age 15, William R. Coe began his ascent up the ladder of Johnson and Higgins, a marine insurance firm (known for underwriting the hull of the *Titanic*). He became president 26 years later and chairman of the board at age 47. Coe's financial situation was certainly not hurt in 1900 when he married his second wife, Mai Huttleston Rogers, daughter of Henry Rogers, one of the founders of Standard Oil.

Coe spared no expense when it came to his beloved estate—his love of the outdoors led to the creation of one of the greatest collections of plants and flowers anywhere in the region. The property's signature tree, a Fairhaven Beech, was shipped from Coe's wife's childhood home and remains there today.

In 1949, Coe sold Coe Hall to the state of New York for a buck. Today, Planting Fields Arboretum is filled with 409 acres of walking trails and horticultural delights. Summer concerts are a big draw, and the arboretum remains one of Long Island's most picturesque and popular attractions.

Coe Hall

William R. Coe (*right*), photographed in 1927, was a self-made man who worked his way up the corporate ladder of a marine insurance firm to become one of the region's wealthiest men. He sold Coe Hall (*above*), his magnificent North Shore estate, to the state of New York for one dollar.

Planting Fields

Planting Fields Arboretum, shown in 2006, features more than 400 acres of unique plant life spread throughout rich gardens and woodland trails. Its greenhouse consists of rare plants from around the Long Island region.

The 65-room Coe family residence remains the centerpiece of the Locust Valley property. Today, it acts as a museum with more than 200 events planned each year that bring the past to life. At left, the garden is shown circa 1930.

GREAT NECK

Great Neck is one of the region's better-known and oldest residential communities. During the early 20th century, Great Neck was a land of incredible wealth. As the railhead of the New York and Flushing Railroad, Great Neck became one of Long Island's first commuter neighborhoods when city residents started moving east to escape the urban hustle and bustle.

Great Neck became known for attracting a roll call of who's-who, celebrities preferring the "country life" while still having easy access to the city. Sid Caesar, the Marx Brothers, W. C. Fields, F. Scott Fitzgerald, Paul Newman, Francis Ford Coppola, and so many others once called Great Neck home.

Through the years, Great Neck has also become a place of strong ethnic ties. After World War II, many Jews migrated in from New York, seeking more land and a better way of life. The new Great Neck residents formed temples and synagogues and pushed for stringent educational policies in the community's schools. This rich Jewish culture still exists in the community today, and the area's public school system is constantly ranked among the best in the country.

In the 1980s, an influx of Iranian Jews came to the area following the 1979 Islamic Revolution. The Iranian community built their own Mizrahi temples and synagogues where they could follow their own traditions.

Today, Great Neck's Village Green, with its historic clock tower along Middle Neck Road, is a historic and culturally diverse downtown area. Hundreds of shops featuring the food, clothes, culture, and style from the melting pot of ethnicities in the community are dispersed throughout.

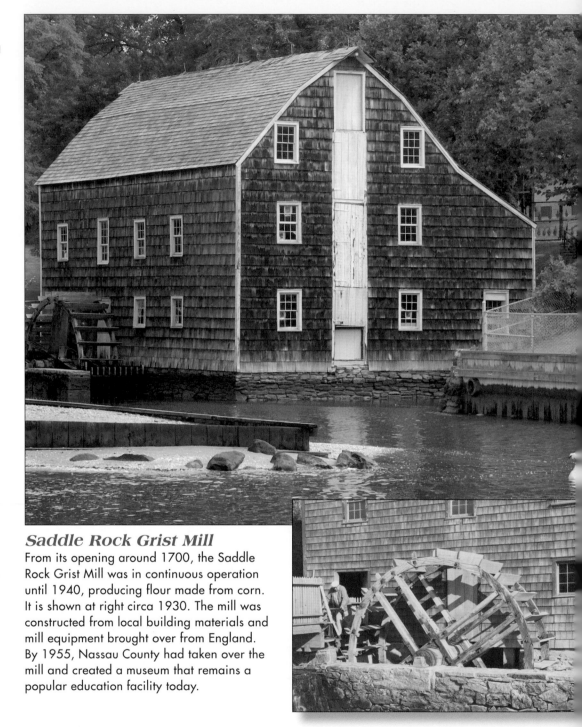

Saddle Rock Grist Mill

From its opening around 1700, the Saddle Rock Grist Mill was in continuous operation until 1940, producing flour made from corn. It is shown at right circa 1930. The mill was constructed from local building materials and mill equipment brought over from England. By 1955, Nassau County had taken over the mill and created a museum that remains a popular education facility today.

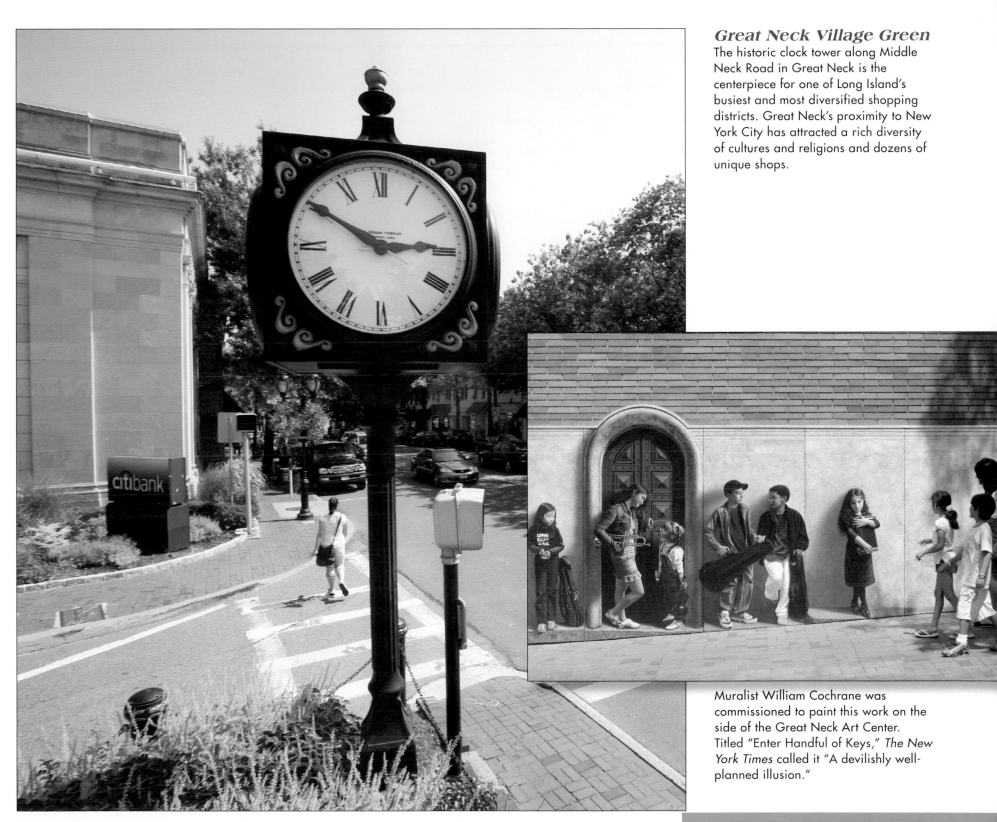

Great Neck Village Green

The historic clock tower along Middle Neck Road in Great Neck is the centerpiece for one of Long Island's busiest and most diversified shopping districts. Great Neck's proximity to New York City has attracted a rich diversity of cultures and religions and dozens of unique shops.

Muralist William Cochrane was commissioned to paint this work on the side of the Great Neck Art Center. Titled "Enter Handful of Keys," *The New York Times* called it "A devilishly well-planned illusion."

MANSION RUINS

After World War I, the Gold Coast became a haven for wealthy investors, bankers, and anybody else with money enough to afford an extravagant lifestyle. Estates grew large and ornate; owners employed small armies of servants who cooked, cleaned, and maintained the grounds (and this is despite the fact that many of these estates were used only as getaway palaces for the summer and/or weekends).

As the calendar turned over to 1929, so did the fortunes of the Gold Coast elite. Black Friday hit and the stock market crashed violently, taking many estate owners down with it. The majority of these land barons had their wealth tied to the stock market. This quick and unforeseen financial plummet forced many Gold Coast mansions to be sold, auctioned, or abandoned.

While many of these properties were reconstructed for different uses, others were razed to make way for more modest homes on smaller building lots. Others still were abandoned and eventually dilapidated, leaving ruins that still permeate the Long Island landscape.

While the Roland Conklin Estate burned down years ago, portions remain of Rosemary Farm. A clock tower, which was part of the old carriage house, still exists. The unique 1918 amphitheater used for outdoor plays and operas has been fully restored—including its surrounding bridge and moat. And though J. P. Morgan's estate at Matinecock Point was demolished in 1980, the bridge still stands—a bridge used in 1915 by a would-be assassin. Morgan suffered two gunshot wounds but survived the attack.

Westbrook Farm/Knollwood Ruins

Treasure hunters and historians can have a field day seeking out the scores of mansion ruins which still exist on the Gold Coast. Seen above are some of the garden pillar remains of "Knollwood," an estate built around 1910 for Charles Hudson in Muttontown.

Laurelton Hall

Louis Comfort Tiffany's estate, Laurelton Hall in Laurel Hollow, was another Long Island mansion that unfortunately fell into disrepair. The minaret (*left*) was used as a chimney. The home's Daffodil Terrace (*above left*), shown in 1924, was on display during an exhibit at the Metropolitan Museum of Art (*above*). At far left are some of the estate's actual Tiffany windows that were part of the same exhibit.

SEA CLIFF

Long Island's topography, for the most part, is flat. But at the Village of Sea Cliff, stunning heights along with hilly and wooded streets provide breathtaking views of Hempstead Harbor and the Long Island Sound. Combine the visual landscape with some of Long Island's most unique Victorian architecture, and Sea Cliff is one of the region's most sought after communities to live in and visit.

There are more than 100 structures highlighting every late Victorian style, from iron-crested mansard roofing to bracketed Carpenter Gothic houses adorned with fretwork. In the 1870s, Sea Cliff was utilized as a religious retreat by a Methodist organization that built a huge tabernacle and campground atop the cliff.

Many of these weekend visitors fell in love with the beautiful scenery of the community and built summer and then permanent homes in the village. Sea Cliff was incorporated in 1883, making it the fourth-oldest village on Long Island and one of the oldest in New York. One of Sea Cliff's early residents was poet and journalist William Cullen Bryant, who commuted to New York City by ship.

Today, through the efforts of the village government to maintain the community's historic architecture, Sea Cliff is a popular place for day-trippers to window shop along Sea Cliff Avenue and walk the streets, marveling at the bright and diversified colors of the Victorian homes that dot the landscape. Residents enjoy the meticulously maintained downtown area, the strip of beach at the base of the cliff, and the 16 parks spread throughout the community.

The unique Victorian architecture of Sea Cliff dating to the late 1800s and early 1900s is still seen in more than 100 homes throughout the North Shore in eastern Nassau County.

Sea Cliff's view takes in breathtaking vistas of the Long Island Sound and the Connecticut coastline. At left is a view of Sea Cliff taken from the Connecticut shoreline in 1903. Sea Cliff was originally founded as a Methodist retreat in the 1870s but, through the years, has drawn many wealthy Manhattanites who enjoy the proximity to the water and the unique views.

The Rocky Coast Along the Historic Sound

While firmly established as a place with hundreds of diversified communities, Long Island is probably best identified by its two coasts—the North and South shores. Created by glaciers tens of thousands of years ago and bordering the Long Island Sound, the North Shore (known for its rocky coast) is a coastal paradise. The area is a haven for those who prefer the tranquility of the sound to the more volatile waves and whitecaps of the South Shore.

Long Island's rich history along the North Shore stretches from eastern Nassau County to Eastern Suffolk. Geographically, the first major North Shore stop in eastern Nassau is Oyster Bay, the area Teddy Roosevelt chose to raise his family and create the "Summer White House." Today, the abode is a national museum named Sagamore Hill; its decor is a testament to Roosevelt's love of the outdoors, with its assortment of animal hides and heads. (Next to his desk, Roosevelt actually used a hollowed-out elephant foot as a wastebasket.)

SCIENTIFIC DISCOVERY TAKES HOLD

Farther east in Cold Spring Harbor is the world-renowned Cold Spring Harbor Laboratory. The lab was created in 1890 as an educational campus to study the ecology of organisms in surrounding water. It still operates today as a place where scientists and researchers from around the world gather to present findings and study human health. Since its creation, the lab has produced seven Nobel Prize winners, but is probably most recognizable as the place where DNA's double-helix structure was

This 1900 picture of Woodbine Avenue in Northport shows its close proximity to Northport Harbor. The buildings on the left have been demolished and now two waterfront parks exist on the site. The largest building on the right is the Thompson Law Book Publishing Company; today the building houses upscale business lofts.

Huntington Village has contained one of Long Island's liveliest downtown districts since the late 1800s. Shown at left is the 250th anniversary celebration of the founding of the community that took place in 1903. The O. S. Sammis Insurance Company, seen in the background, stood at the corner of Main Street and New York Avenue. The Sammis family continues in the insurance and real estate businesses in the area to this day.

a testament to the community's Native American past.

FROM LAND TO SEA
The fishing and seafaring history of Long Island's North Shore touches most of its coastal communities in one form or another. Northport's Main Street runs down a mile-long hill until it reaches Northport Harbor. The trolley-car tracks, the common mode of travel in the early 20th century, can still be seen set in the roadway, although the trolley no longer functions.

A little farther east, the popular tourist destination of Port Jefferson features the Bridgeport & Port Jefferson Steamboat Company, which, you guessed it, connects Long Island to Bridgeport, Connecticut. While currently a trendy area filled with restaurants and shops, Port Jefferson was the largest shipbuilding center in Suffolk County in the 1800s.

Beyond the obvious historic structures and odes to the sea, the North Shore today is known for its tranquil neighborhoods and expensive real estate. Residents enjoy the suburban life, surrounded by many historic homes, museums, churches, and other legacies of the past. The efforts of many historical societies have been successful in ensuring that a piece of the past remains prevalent and functioning in today's world.

The Bayville Bridge connects the North Shore village of Mill Neck to Bayville over Oyster Bay Harbor. The bridge shown here was opened in 1938, but it is actually the fourth bridge built on or near the site; the others opened in 1898, 1904, and 1922. The current bridge is a 525-foot-long drawbridge.

originally discovered by Dr. James Watson and his team of researchers. Downtown Cold Spring Harbor dazzles visitors with an eyeful of Dickens-esque architecture, drawing window shoppers to walk the quaint streets and browse the village shops, some of which date to the late 1800s.

A PIECE OF AMERICANA
Crossing into Suffolk County, downtown Huntington enchants with its own sense of Main Street Americana. While its history dates back to the Revolutionary War, Huntington today has been honored by the National Civic League as an "All-American City" for its livability, historic preservation, and natural resources. A journey south into West Hills reveals the Walt Whitman Homestead. Whitman, often referred to as America's Poet Laureate, was born in the area in 1819.

America's oldest (and still operating) general store opened in St. James in 1857. The area's bygone past remains alive through historic demonstrations and the selling of antiques. St. James abuts one of Long Island's most aesthetically compelling communities, Nissequogue. With just 1,000 residents, the waterside neighborhood is filled with historic homes and horse farms.

Connected to this idyllic village is the Town of Smithtown, one of the region's best-kept historic enclaves. The downtown district features a number of historic buildings including a tavern, cottage, and brush farm all dating from the 1700s. The First Presbyterian Church was built in the late 1600s and still draws parishioners to its pews each Sunday. Welcoming visitors to Smithtown is the iconic "Smithtown Bull." Erected on May 10, 1941, it has stood as

Beyond the fact that it is one of the world's foremost research laboratories, Cold Spring Harbor Laboratory also features an eclectic mix of architectural styles and artwork spread throughout its campus.

Roosevelt spent 34 years of his life (1885–1919) at his beloved Oyster Bay residence, Sagamore Hill. He died there in 1919 and is buried in nearby Youngs Memorial Cemetery.

SAGAMORE HILL

Former President Theodore "Teddy" Roosevelt is probably Long Island's most famous resident. On summer trips to the Oyster Bay area during the 1870s, Roosevelt (then a teenager living in Manhattan) fell in love with the region's natural habitats. Upon graduating from college, he purchased a plot of land and decided to build on Long Island.

However, tragedy struck Roosevelt in 1884 while he was still working on sketches of the new home. His wife, Alice, died just two days after giving birth to the couple's first child (also named Alice). Although grief stricken, Roosevelt decided to soldier on with his plans.

The 23-room home, called Sagamore Hill, was built on an 83-acre site for just under $17,000; Roosevelt moved there in 1885 and remarried in 1886. With his second wife, Edith, he raised six children in Oyster Bay; Roosevelt called those years the best of his life.

After he became the country's 26th president (following the assassination of William McKinley), Roosevelt made Sagamore Hill his "Summer White House." Every year, he would retreat from the stress of Washington to spend time with his children.

Roosevelt died in his sleep in the Gate Room of his beloved Sagamore Hill in 1919 at the age of 60; he's buried in Oyster Bay's Youngs Memorial Cemetery, only a mile away. His wife continued to reside at Sagamore Hill until her death in 1948.

In 1962, Congress established Sagamore Hill as a National Historic Site, and today Roosevelt's home stands nearly as it did more than a century ago. His love of the outdoors is prevalent throughout the home's furnishings and in the hunting trophies that adorn the walls. Sagamore Hill is now a popular tourist attraction, drawing tens of thousands of visitors each year.

Sagamore Hill (*above*) was referred to as the "Summer White House" when Roosevelt was president. This vintage photo of the Trophy Room (*left*) at Sagamore Hill shows Roosevelt's love of big game hunting. Teddy netted some incredible prizes on African safaris. The Trophy Room remains intact for visitors to view.

Roosevelt conducted much of the business of the country from his front porch at Sagamore Hill. Shown here is a 1904 photo of Roosevelt and the Republican National Committee, taken toward the end of his first term as president.

THEODORE ROOSEVELT

ROOSEVELT WAS A TRUE renaissance man. He was a war hero, the author of more than 25 books, and the creator of the National Collegiate Athletic Association. Roosevelt was also the first sitting president to win the Nobel Peace Prize, which he was awarded for mediating an end to the Russo-Japanese War. The treaty was signed on Sagamore Hill's porch.

Theodore Roosevelt Memorial Park

More than 5,000 people attended the opening of Theodore Roosevelt Memorial Park in 1928.
Today it remains a picturesque and popular location for local Oyster Bay residents.

COLD SPRING HARBOR LABORATORY

The world-renowned Cold Spring Harbor Laboratory (CSHL) came to the North Shore in the late 1800s as an offshoot of the Brooklyn Institute of Arts and Sciences' biology laboratory for high school and college teachers. Needing a coastal environment to study plant and animal life in their natural habitat, the institute's leadership selected Cold Spring Harbor.

After a donation of land and buildings by John D. Jones, the biological lab held its first class in 1890. Its original mission centered on teaching biological sciences, but CSHL has since evolved into a worldwide leader in the study of genetics, cancer, and other disease research.

In 1928, studies centered on finding a genetic basis for cancer. By World War II, a bacterial virus course was developed that sparked the first training of molecular biologists in the country.

Still, CSHL is best known for its DNA research. In 1952, experiments conducted by two CSHL scientists—Alfred D. Hershey and Martha Chase—led to the discovery of DNA as the molecule of heredity. A year later, James Watson and Francis Crick presented their model of the double helix structure at a CSHL symposium. Their research won the Nobel Prize, one of seven that the lab's scientists and researchers have won over the years.

Research during the '60s centered on genetics. In 1968, Watson became lab director; he refocused the lab's objectives on cancer research and viral studies. Research programs have expanded to include neurosciences and genomic studies, ushering in a modern era of biological discoveries.

The lab is now an accredited doctoral-granting institution and is one of the most important centers for cell, cancer, and AIDS research in the entire world.

Shown above is the main building on the campus circa 1905. At right is lab director (and 1969 Nobel Prize winner) Alfred D. Hershey in 1959.

While this picturesque view may look like a New England village, it is actually the Cold Spring Harbor Laboratory campus. The campus houses more than 400 scientists conducting ground-breaking research in diseases, bioinformatics, and plant genetics.

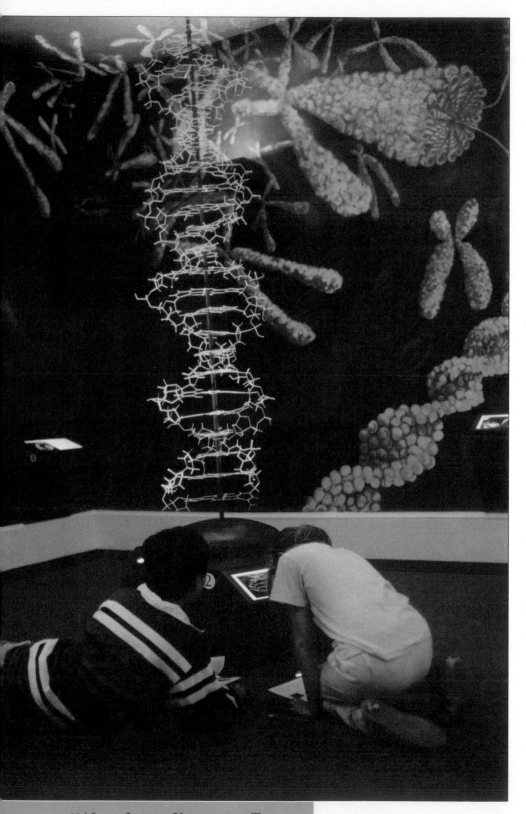

DNA Learning Center

The double helix shape of DNA was discovered at Cold Spring Harbor Laboratory and has a constant presence at the lab's Learning Center.

The Cold Spring Harbor Lighthouse was built in 1890 at the entrance of Cold Spring Harbor about a quarter mile from Centre Island. After being abandoned in 1965 by the Coast Guard, it was purchased by a local resident who moved it into his yard, where it still stands.

Jones Laboratory

The technology and times may have been different, but scientific experiments and discovery have been going on at Cold Spring Harbor for more than 100 years. Built in 1890, the Jones Laboratory is one of the original campus buildings.

HUNTINGTON VILLAGE

While Huntington's past can be traced to its settlement in 1653, its formative period didn't begin until the American Revolution. British forces used Huntington as a local head-quarters and treated the area like any imperialist does its subjects—troops were known for pillaging farms, forcing servitude, and desecrating a local cemetery (Old Burying Hill, which still rests behind the current town historian's office).

But local rebels resisted, drawing the ire of the redcoats. In 1776, Nathan Hale came to Huntington on a spying mission directed by General George Washington; he was captured and later executed. A monument in Halesite honors his life.

The best-known symbol of those difficult times from the revolution still stands at the Old First Presbyterian Church. A 550-pound bell, bearing the town's name and cast in London, was taken by the British in 1777 and used on armed British brigs throughout the war. In 1783, when Huntington town

leaders discovered the bell's location on the East River, they petitioned the British for its return. The bell came back to Huntington with the words "The Town Endures" inscribed inside. It rang from the church's belfry until 1967 when it was retired.

The 250th anniversary of Huntington's founding was celebrated with a visit from President Teddy Roosevelt on July 4, 1903. Business in the region continued to grow during the early 20th century and with it came innovation. Joseph Cantrell is said to have invented the station wagon in 1915 at his carriage shop; Fred Waller invented water skis at his factory in 1925.

Like much of Long Island, Huntington's population exploded after World War II, forcing the downtown area to grow. Huntington's shopping district remains one of Long Island's largest and busiest. In 2002, Huntington was honored as an All-American City.

With its dirt roads and horse-powered transportation, Main Street in Huntington had a very different feel than it does now. This photo was taken in 1907, over 100 years ago.

This 1939 view of Main Street looking west (*above*) takes in the bustling downtown that was and is Huntington. Modern-day Huntington (*right*) remains a popular place for those who prefer the small town outdoor shopping experience.

Thimble Factory

Shown above during the mid-19th century, Ezra C. Prime's thimble factory was located in downtown Huntington. Established in 1836, the factory was described as the largest of its kind in the country; Prime ran it for more than 40 years.

Huntington Harbor

Sailing on present-day Huntington Harbor remains quite popular with Long Island's North Shore residents who continue to moor their boats from Memorial Day through the summer season in full view of the Coindre Hall boathouse. At left, circa 1925, is the Walter E. Abrams Shipyard, adjacent to Huntington Harbor. Shipbuilding and repair was one of the area's leading industries of the time.

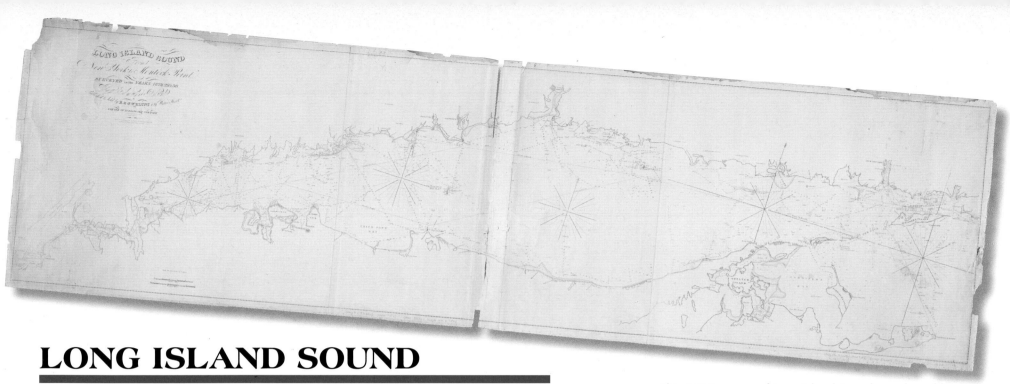

LONG ISLAND SOUND

This 1828 survey of Long Island Sound, conducted by Edmund Blunt, provides a prime view of the jagged nature of the land along Long Island's North Shore.

Separating Long Island and Connecticut with distances ranging from 5 to 19 miles, the Long Island Sound is an estuary where fresh water from rivers mix with salt water from the ocean. The sound connects to the East River in New York City to the west and to Block Island Sound to the east; it covers more than 600 miles of coastline, including Connecticut's South Shore, pieces of Queens and the Bronx, and parts of Westchester County.

Since its discovery in 1614 by explorer Adriaen Block, the sound has provided Long Islanders with entertainment and employment. Residents of many ports on the Long Island side have used the northern coast as a place to build boats, fish, and swim; waterfront property along the sound is some of the most valuable in the country.

As development and population shifts have occurred, there have been a string of proposals regarding the construction of a cross-sound bridge or tunnel. In the 1960s, master builder Robert Moses proposed a bridge from Rye to Oyster Bay that Governor Nelson Rockefeller shot down. More recently, a Sound Tunnel has been proposed to help provide better egress off the island. But due to traffic, cost, and political and environmental concerns, those plans never went forward.

Like most waterways, the Long Island Sound is a delicate ecosystem. It features myriad plant and animal life and more than 120 species of fish in its waters, and environmentalists closely monitor its pollution levels. With large cities like Bridgeport and New Haven and hundreds of thousands of Long Island residents residing along its coasts, it is essential for the sound to maintain a balance between development, progress, and environmental stability.

Considered one of the fastest steamers of its time, the *Lexington* caught fire and sank near the Eaton's Neck Lighthouse on January 13, 1840. The accident, one of the worst in the history of Long Island Sound, killed 154 passengers and crew.

Above: Crab Meadow Beach in Huntington was a popular family place in 1940. This dog show drew many to the boardwalk during a warm summer Sunday.

Left: Written in 1912 by Earle C. Jones and Charles N. Daniels, the song "On Long Island Sound" was an ode to the sand and sea so popular with the beachgoers of the day.

This tranquil scene from the cliffs of the North Shore west of Port Jefferson captures another summer day on Long Island.

This photo of Main Street in Northport was taken around 1900. The marchers on the left are Civil War veterans. The trolley car tracks still exist on Main Street today, even though there are no operating trolleys.

NORTHPORT VILLAGE

Downtown Northport's history can be traced along one historic path. From the tip of Main Street leading to Northport Harbor are trolley tracks—tracks that transported travelers from the Northport train station to the village throughout the first quarter of the 20th century.

Northport began humbly as a farming community called Great Cow Harbor; in 1830, there were only eight dwellings in the area. However, a burgeoning shipbuilding industry was sparked by the area's coastal location, and by the late 1830s the area was referred to as Northport.

Jump ahead to 1875, when Northport had six general stores, two hotels, and three shipbuilders. Shipbuilding kept the region bustling until the turn of the century when the wooden ships being produced in Northport began to be replaced by more durable and modern steel-hulled ships.

By the 1920s, after nearly 100 years of heavy commercial use, the waterfront had fallen into a state of decay. Village officials purchased land along the harbor and created Northport Memorial Park in 1932. That set the stage for the idyllic waterfront setting that still exists today. In 1958, at age 36, author, poet, and pioneer of the beat generation Jack Kerouac moved to Northport to care for his mother and seek seclusion from his newfound acclaim. The pub he frequented on Main Street is now a local landmark.

Contemporary Northport is a quaint seaside community of unique shops, restaurants, waterfront docks, parks, and activities. The village is popular with residents and visitors who marvel at the many church steeples lining Main Street and enjoy the unobstructed sunset views.

Jones Drug Store

Jones Drug Store remains a fixture on Northport's Main Street today. The photo at left shows the store as it looked in 1910.

John W. Engeman Theater

Northport's first theater opened on Main Street in 1912, but it burned down in 1932. The current theater was built next to the original site and operated for more than 60 years, mostly as a movie house until it closed in the late 1990s. Today, the building is home to the John W. Engeman Theater, named for the new owner's brother who was killed in Iraq. The theater opened in 2007 to rave reviews.

At the end of Main Street is the Northport Pier, a popular place for a summer stroll to watch a sunset or the boats coming in. The fisherman statue (*above*) used to greet visitors to the area until the crack in its head grew too large. With its head split in half, the statue was removed.

STONY BROOK VILLAGE

The bucolic look of the Stony Brook Village Center was the brainchild of Ward Melville (*right*), founder of the Thom McAn Shoe Company. At his own expense, Melville, an influential area resident, had the center remodeled in 1940–41.

The arrival of philanthropist Ward Melville to Stony Brook Village can be considered serendipitous. His parents, Frank and Jennie, boarded the wrong train, and instead of arriving in the Hamptons as they planned, they found themselves in the little-known village. At the time (the early 1930s) Stony Brook was run down, cluttered with declining commercial buildings and stores. Yet Ward found charm in the village, and he had the money and generosity to see that charm transformed.

Between 1940 and 1941, the Stony Brook Village Center was completely reconstructed and remodeled at Ward's expense. (Melville is also the founder of the Thom McAn Shoe Company.) The crescent-shape center and assorted shops were constructed around a Federal-Greek Revival style post office. In the post office's pediment is a mechanical eagle that has flapped its wings—every hour on the hour—from 8 A.M. to 8 P.M. since 1941. The area is considered to be the first planned shopping center in the country.

In 1947, Melville also acquired the Stony Brook Grist Mill, which was originally built in 1751. It was restored and still operates today as a tourist site and an educational center for school children. Melville, who was very generous to his beloved community, also donated the land that would become Stony Brook University.

Today, the Village Center remains a popular shopping and dining attraction. To honor Melville's legacy, the local high school bears his name.

The Stony Brook Grist Mill, built in 1751, has been renovated and remodeled over the years and still operates as an educational center for children and a popular tourist spot. Throwing bread to the ducks in the surrounding pond is a favorite activity for visitors.

FIRST RADIO BROADCAST

The first transatlantic radio message originated from RCA Radio Central in Rocky Point, located along the North Shore of Suffolk County. In 1921, President Warren G. Harding pressed a button to originate the message from the White House; the message then traveled from Rocky Point to Europe using long-wave signals.

The first transatlantic commercial phone service also came from Rocky Point. Radio Central was a huge facility, consisting of 12 transmitting towers, each standing 412 feet high. The total site stretches over 6,400 acres and was built between 1919 and 1920.

RCA also conducted research and technological experiments from its ten buildings scattered across the property. During one of its "secret" experiments, color television was first developed. As technological changes came quickly after World War II and short-wave replaced long-wave transmissions, the site's usefulness diminished, and the property was sold to the state of New York for $1 in the early 1970s.

Today, the RCA site is the largest tract of land located within the Long Island Pine Barrens. Hikers, hunters, and mountain bikers have access to a portion of the property.

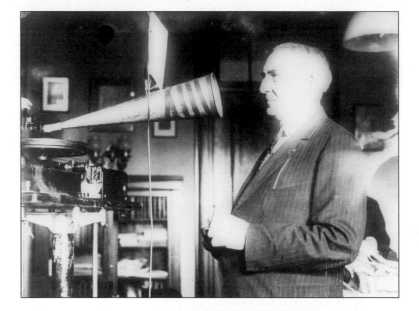

The first transatlantic message ever sent was delivered from RCA Radio Central in Rocky Point in 1921. Shown is President Warren G. Harding speaking into an early recording device.

Rocky Point was the center of the radio world in the early 1900s. Shown is General Electric engineer E.F.W. Alexanderson with one of the high-frequency alternators he developed at the site.

This pristine piece of land, which once housed the RCA radio site, is now known as Pine Barrens and is one of Long Island's largest tracts of undeveloped land. The site remains a popular destination for hikers and nature lovers.

In the 1920s, RCA's 6,400 acres housed 12 radio towers—each standing more than 400 feet tall—making the eastern section of Long Island's North Shore the epicenter for new technology in communication.

TESLA TOWER

WHEN YOU THINK OF controversial historical figures, inventors rarely come to mind. That isn't the case with Nikola Tesla, whose life (as well as his legacy) was—pun intended—a lightning rod for controversy. Though oftentimes considered a mad scientist because of his support and work in pseudoscience and UFO speculation, Tesla was one of the inventors responsible not only for commercial electricity, but also for the invention of radio (the U.S. Supreme Court awarded him the credit in 1943).

One of Tesla's most controversial and ambitious projects took place on Long Island at Wardenclyffe Tower. It was here that Tesla experimented in wireless telecommunications and on his notorious "death ray."

The tower, which occupied 200 acres of land owned by James S. Warden, was never completed due to funding difficulties. And Tesla's death ray? The key components were allegedly stolen by Russian spies, though the FBI denies ever finding the schematics.

Port Jefferson Village was still a bustling shipbuilding and shipping center when this photo of Main Street (looking south) was taken around 1920.

PORT JEFFERSON

One of Long Island's most picturesque and popular villages is Port Jefferson. Located along the Long Island Sound, the seaside village attracts day-trippers who ferry in from Bridgeport, Connecticut, and tourists who shop the hundreds of downtown stores and enjoy the historic sightseeing opportunities.

Originally named Drowned Meadow, the village was renamed after President Thomas Jefferson in 1836. Jefferson helped secure funds to dredge the harbor, furthering the shipbuilding business. Seamen, whalers, and boatbuilders made up the vast percentage of the population during the 1800s. At its peak in 1850, the village boasted 12 shipbuilding companies. In 1852, after the village was named an American port of entry, a customs house was constructed on Main Street. That building still stands, though the street has changed its name to High Street.

Port Jefferson's bustling downtown traces its roots to 1836. The road built from upper Port Jefferson was where many businesses sprouted to serve the shipbuilders and seamen living in the area.

The ferry line from Port Jefferson to Bridgeport has been operational since 1883; the village's Mather Shipyard built its first ferry, the *Nonowantuc,* in 1883. One of Bridgeport & Port Jefferson Steamboat Company's stockholders was circus master P. T. Barnum. Barnum, who lived in Connecticut but owned land in Port Jefferson, wanted to use the village as a training center for his circus acts. Residents balked, and Barnum eventually sold his property. Years later, Barnum would get the last laugh when an avenue was named in his honor.

Vestiges of Port Jefferson's shipping past are scattered throughout the village today. This waterfront park's anchor is a popular photo spot. Thousands of boaters use the village docks and piers each summer.

Ferry Lines

Ferrying islanders to and from Connecticut has been going on between Port Jefferson and Bridgeport since 1883. The modern ferries of today (*near right*) certainly seem sleeker and more comfortable for the 90-minute trek than the dated 1950 version (*far right*).

WALT WHITMAN HOMESTEAD

Born in West Hills, Long Island in 1819 in a shingled crafts-man home built by his father, Walt Whitman is one of America's most beloved men of letters.

Whitman's life was not easy. He was the second of nine children, four of whom were handicapped. Because of financial difficulties, the family moved to Brooklyn when Whitman was young, and he was taken out of school at age 11 to help support his family. Without formal schooling, Whitman read the Bible and found inspiration in classic authors such as Homer, Shakespeare, and Dante. Early work in a Brooklyn print shop instilled in him the love of writing and reading.

At 17, he entered the classroom again, this time as a teacher. He soon left that profession and founded the *Long Islander* newspaper (based in Huntington) in 1838 and worked at the *Brooklyn Daily Eagle* as an editor in the 1840s.

Whitman's masterpiece is undoubtedly his collection of poetry, *Leaves of Grass,* which was first published in 1855. (Whitman would update and edit it throughout his life.) The collection, in addition to his other work, was considered controversial at the time because of its sexual themes and political stances.

The Whitman birthplace and homestead museum in West Hills was almost lost to an outside purchaser in 1949. However, an association was formed by New York literary figures, scholars, and citizens to save the home and honor Whitman's legacy. The association donated the property to the state in 1957.

The birthplace site and museum features tours, a walking trail, and artifacts from Whitman's life. Although situated on the bustling Route 110 corridor, the Whitman homesite echoes a literal respite of time, place, and humanity.

Walt Whitman was born in the West Hills home his father built in 1819. This photo (*top*), taken in 1903, shows its dilapidated state. Because of the fund-raising of some concerned Long Islanders, the homestead today is a spruced-up and often-visited site for people interested in Whitman's historic words.

In 1842, Whitman wrote a novel about temperance called *Franklin Evans*, predating his masterpiece, the poetry collection *Leaves of Grass*, by 13 years. His use of free verse and cadence styles astounded his contemporaries, including Ralph Waldo Emerson. Seen above is the Whitman Interpretaive Center.

ST. JAMES GENERAL STORE

The St. James General Store is the oldest continuously operating general store in the United States. Ebenezer Smith opened the store in its current location in 1857.

During the store's early years, its location was in the heart of downtown St. James, a farming community with about 30 residences; it was a place where people could buy medicine, groceries, tobacco, yard goods, and kitchenware. Because the post office was there, the store also became a meeting place for locals to gossip.

The St. James General Store was also the first place in the community to have a telephone, allowing it to maintain its unofficial status as a community center. Renowned architect Stanford White, a local resident, was said to conduct business from the store's telephone.

In the late 1800s, Ebenezer passed the store on to his son, Everett, who continued to run it until his death in 1940. The store was sold to several other owners until 1990, all of whom made efforts to preserve its historic nature. In 1990, Suffolk County and the state of New York purchased the general store and their combined efforts keep it functioning.

The store, which is listed on the National Register of Historic Places, operates as it did from 1880 to 1900: as a seller of antique and general store products. The employees dress in period garb, and the goods are placed in bins and on shelves dating back to the 1800s. The upstairs now functions as a bookstore, featuring craft demonstrations, readings, and educational programs for children and adults.

The St. James General Store of today may be more colorful on the outside, but the structure remains intact. The store's exterior sign and an American flag have greeted shoppers since its opening.

This postcard shows off the St. James General Store. It is considered the oldest establishment of its kind in the country. The front porch was the community's gathering place to collect mail and swap gossip.

At the St. James General Store, patrons can still buy many of the types of food and home goods that were available more than 150 years ago. The Indian statue greets visitors while providing a remembrance of the strong Native American influence that exists throughout the Long Island region.

CARRIAGE MUSEUM

The country's finest collection of historic horse-drawn carriages is located at the Long Island Museum of American Art, History and Carriages in Stony Brook Village. There are ten unique galleries housing the museum's collection of more than 200 horse-drawn carriages (though only 100 are on display at a time) as well as artifacts from this period of American history when carriages were the common means of transportation.

The institution is the largest privately supported museum on Long Island and features every type of carriage imaginable, from stagecoaches to live-in carriages to firefighting wagons (and even carriages designed for children). The museum recently welcomed a new addition—an authentic 19th century carriage-making shop that was relocated from Williamsburg, Massachusetts.

The art museum features more than 4,000 pieces, including the work of renowned genre artist and local resident William Sidney Mount. The history museum showcases Long Island's place in America from the 17th century through the 1930s. Special exhibits highlight the region's nautical past.

In 2006, the Long Island Museum became a Smithsonian affiliate; the honor grants the museum extensive resources and unique research opportunities.

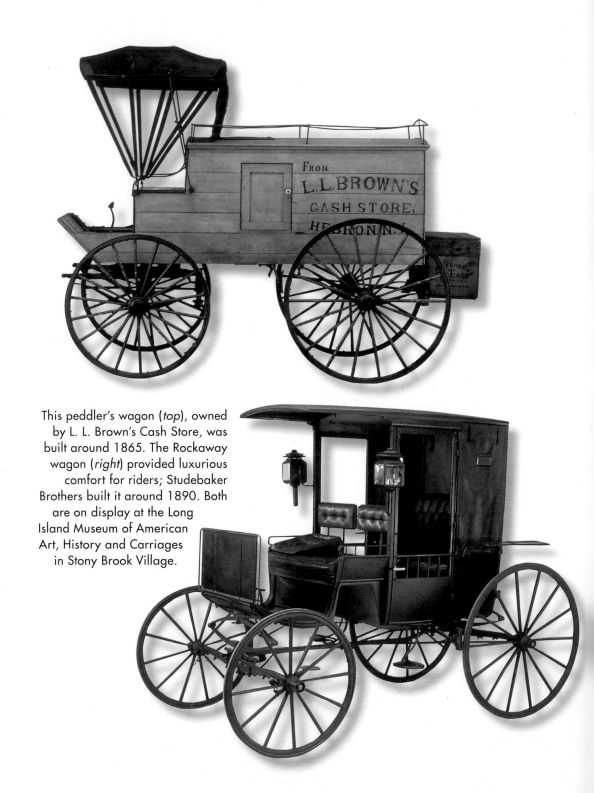

This peddler's wagon (*top*), owned by L. L. Brown's Cash Store, was built around 1865. The Rockaway wagon (*right*) provided luxurious comfort for riders; Studebaker Brothers built it around 1890. Both are on display at the Long Island Museum of American Art, History and Carriages in Stony Brook Village.

In addition to its impressive collection of more than 200 period carriages, the museum features over 40,000 historical pieces from the 18th century and beyond that provide an in-depth look at life on Long Island.

SMITHTOWN BULL

The 14-foot, 5-ton bronze statue of Whisper, the Smithtown Bull, has regally welcomed visitors to Smithtown since 1941.

The legend of the bull, however, dates all the way back to the late 1600s when Richard Smith supposedly rescued the kidnapped daughter of a local Native American chief. The chief was so thankful for Smith's deed that he offered to grant title to all of the land Smith could encircle on a bull in one day. The land he covered is what is said to be Smithtown.

Getting the bull statue to its current site was a little complicated. The concept for the bull statue dates back to 1903 when Lawrence Smith Butler, a direct descendent of Richard Smith, proposed the idea. Charles Cary Rumsey, a sculptor and acquaintance of Butler, was commissioned to create the statue for a price of $12,000.

The casting of the bull statue was not completed until 1923, after which the finished statue sat outside the Brooklyn Museum for several years and then was placed in storage because of a funding shortage.

Finally, in 1941, Butler "convinced the Town Board to build a concrete pedestal to hold the statue, raised the $1,750 needed to cover the cost of the move, and convinced Rumsey's heirs to donate the statue to the Town." And on May 10, 1941, the daughter of the sculptor and first lady of the state of New York, Mary Rumsey, presented the statue to Smithtown's residents.

Today, the statue remains a well-known and beloved figure representing the vast history of Smithtown.

Legend has it that Bread and Cheese Hollow Road is named for the location Richard Smith stopped for lunch on his apocryphal "claiming" of Smithtown.

Caleb Smith House

The Caleb Smith House, which was originally built in 1819 on the Jericho Turnpike, was moved to its present location on North Country Road in 1955. The photo at left shows the house around 1940.

Obadiah Smith House

At the rear of the Obadiah Smith house is a ten-foot-wide fireplace, the stone backside of which makes up the residence's back end. When the house was built around 1700, that was a very unusual feature. The 853-foot site was given to Obadiah by Richard Smith, his grandfather and Smithtown founder.

FIRST PRESBYTERIAN CHURCH

As is the case with most things in Smithtown, the First Presbyterian Church exists only because of the generosity of the town's patriarch. In 1675, Richard Smith not only donated the land on which the church would be built, but he also fronted the money for its construction. Back then, the church was located near the Nissequogue River, close to the area's meetinghouse.

As the downtown area of Smithtown grew and eventually shifted, the church was relocated in 1750 to its current site directly across from the Smithtown Library. The new land was donated by Obadiah and Epenetus Smith. At the time of the church's move, the preacher was Reverend Napthali Daggett, a man who would go on to become a professor and, eventually, the sixth president of Yale University.

During the Revolutionary War, British soldiers fired on then-pastor Joshua Hartt, who was preaching from the pulpit. Hartt was taken to New York City and imprisoned for his "inflammatory" sermons.

After the dust had settled from the war, the church was officially incorporated in 1794. But the church population was still growing; a new and expanded building was dedicated in 1827. The building has since been expanded to include a Sunday school, lecture rooms, and offices. In 1977, the church was added to the National Register of Historic Places.

Through the years, the First Presbyterian Church has been able to preserve its history with commemorative plaques, photos, and historical documents—all of which are displayed throughout the church's interior.

From Shipwrecks and Buccaneers to Breezy Ocean Living

What is it about a white, sandy beach that is so appealing? Is it the ocean breezes? The coastal sounds? The crashing whitecaps? The brilliant sunshine? On Long Island the answer is simple: all of the above.

The South Shore of Long Island filters east from Long Beach in Nassau County to Bellport in Suffolk County. Along that 65-mile stretch, one thing is ever-present: water. And with that comes much of what draws people to the region—sand, surf, fishing, boating, and coastal living.

Off the southern coast of Long Island, the 45-mile-long Great South Bay separates the mainland from Fire Island. A calm haven before the rugged waters of the huge ocean to the east, the bay is a popular attraction for fishing boats and recreational boaters alike. It also has a storied nautical history dating back to the 1700s when local lore describes

buccaneers and rumrunners, including the infamous Blackbeard and Captain Morgan, causing havoc along the coastal waters of Bay Shore and Freeport.

FIRE ISLAND

East of the Great South Bay, Fire Island is a 31-mile-long barrier island on Long Island's South Shore, situated adjacent to the Atlantic Ocean. The vast majority of the island is protected by the Fire Island National Seashore and filled with disparate communities that attract thousands of summertime tourists and residents. Due to limited vehicle access, there are less than a thousand year-round residents on Fire Island. The island is only a quarter-mile wide at its thickest point,

This 1908 photo of dredging in Long Beach shows the backbreaking manual labor needed not only to fill in land with earth but also to build Reynolds Channel.

Jones Beach remains one of Long Island's most popular destinations. This 1950s-era photo shows the hundreds of thousands of sunbathers who would travel to the beach on a summer weekend, as evidenced by the packed parking lots. The lower body of calm water is Zach's Bay, with the Jones Beach Amphitheater on the right. In the center is the Jones Beach water tower and behind that the rougher Atlantic Ocean.

It's believed that the first whaling expeditions in the colonies took place in Long Island in 1644. By the mid-1800s (when this photo was taken), whaling was one of the region's most popular, dangerous, and lucrative forms of employment. Here, a group of South Shore whalers remove a whale's skin along an Atlantic Ocean beach—the whale's blubber was the most valuable asset of the catch.

and as a result, Mother Nature continually threatens it. In fact, the Great Hurricane of 1938 caused drastic erosion problems and broke the island away from its original connection point near Shinnecock Bay. Today, Fire Island is mostly accessible by ferries that run from Bay Shore and Sayville.

Fire Island's rich history dates back to 1653 when Isaac Stratford of Babylon constructed Whalehouse Point, a whaling station. Stratford and his crew hauled boats across a narrow sand island to the ocean and built towers to watch for the spouting of a whale. The whalers were then able to track their prey, hoping for the kill that would provide valuable oil and blubber. The Fire Island Lighthouse, the most visible attraction on the island, was constructed in 1825 and is still operational today.

JONES BEACH

When discussing the world's famous beaches, Long Island's Jones Beach is an inveterate part of the conversation. Created by developer and planner Robert Moses, Jones Beach opened on August 4, 1929. As one of the state's first public parks, the oceanfront area covers 6.5 miles along the South Shore of central Nassau. Moses was concerned with what amusements and rides would do to the park's character, so he prohibited them. The prohibition still exists, keeping the area free from development other than its water tower, theater, and two bathhouses.

Today, the west end of the park provides surf fishing, a boat basin, and undeveloped areas that are home to a variety of plants and migratory birds. Jones Beach also hosts the popular Memorial Day weekend air show, which draws 400,000 people; in 1952, its amphitheater was rebuilt from a small outdoor venue to Long Island's most popular rock 'n' roll concert location.

THE RIVIERA OF THE EAST

At the South Shore's westernmost point rests Long Beach, nicknamed "The City by the Sea." Incorporated in 1922, Long Beach has gone through many changes over the years. In the early 1900s, developer William Reynolds had a vision to transform the area into the Riviera of the East. He built hotels and developments in ornate Mediterranean-style architecture, and the area quickly became a popular spot for vacationers. After a period of urban decay and city corruption precipitated by the Great Depression, Long Beach became dilapidated in the 1970s. However, a recent resurgence of new construction and efforts to restore the city's rich history has resulted in the area's revival.

THE PAST, PRESERVED

Long Island's South Shore region is filled with many diverse communities: Babylon, Bay Shore, and Brightwaters in Suffolk County feature channels and canals that lead to the Great South Bay, affording many residents the ability to build a dock in their backyards.

Bellport Village has a historic coastal past, which has been painstakingly preserved as one of the island's most picturesque villages. Its historic district is a popular spot for both history buffs and tourists. In nearby Blue Point, Jacob Ockers, "The Oyster King," was the first to set up an oyster processing plant in 1876. By 1890 there were 25 oyster shanties spread along the South Shore. Blue Point oysters were considered a delicacy by the rich and famous; consequently, they were regularly shipped to the finest restaurants in the world. Over-harvesting and excessive algae growth severely curtailed the size of Long Island's oyster beds by the mid-1900s.

While Long Island's North Shore has always been associated more with the wealthy residents of the region, the South Shore has been the coast of the people. Populated by a more blue-collar and sea-worthy mentality, South Shore residents take great pride in their relationship to the bay and ocean waters.

The Fire Island Bridge, completed in 1964 over Fire Island Inlet, connects Captree Island to Fire Island on Long Island's South Shore. Motorists use it to reach Robert Moses State Park and the Atlantic Ocean beaches or to connect to the Ocean Parkway.

JONES BEACH

Long Island is known for having some of the most beautiful and natural beaches in the world, but a man-made park, Jones Beach State Park, is its most popular coastal attraction.

Jones Beach State Park was the vision of Robert Moses—former president of the New York State Parks Commission—who wanted to build a state park that was free of development and open to the general public. The project began with legislation signed in 1923; after years of laborious construction, Jones Beach opened to rave reviews in 1929.

Moses didn't want just a beach; he wanted a playground the entire public could enjoy—and he got it. Jones Beach features a two-mile boardwalk with food concessions, two bathhouses, a water tower, and numerous other facilities. In 1952, the 8,200-seat Jones Beach Marine Stadium was opened a half-mile north of the main beach. The outdoor theater featured a moat in front of the stage, allowing for watercraft to be part of the productions. Today, though the moat has been built over, the theater has been expanded and modernized to become a 15,200-seat venue.

Moses' original vision for Jones Beach has stood the test of time. After 80 years, it still receives millions of visitors each year and over the course of a hot summer weekend will draw upwards of 250,000 people. The Jones Beach location on the South Shore of Nassau County makes it an easy commute for beachgoers from all over Long Island, New York City, and Westchester County.

Since 2004, the New York Air Show has become one of the most popular of its kind in the country. The show takes place over the Memorial Day weekend and attracts some of the world's best-known flyers, acrobats, and aerialists. The 2009 show drew a record 407,000 visitors over a three-day period.

This 1955 production of *Arabian Nights* at the Jones Beach Amphitheater in Wantagh was one of the many lavish productions that came to the South Shore each summer. Because of the moat that surrounded the theater, productions oftentimes featured elaborate aquatic themes.

The Jones Beach Boardwalk (shown here circa 1937) has been the centerpiece of the park since it opened in 1929. The two-mile stretch features shops and food stands and provides a convenient place for a leisurely stroll.

This Jones Beach brochure was produced in the 1930s for distribution to New York City residents. Before suburbia was born on Long Island in the late 1940s, the majority of beachgoers came to Long Island from points north and west.

JONES BEACH
STATE PARK

LONG ISLAND
STATE PARK
COMMISSION

U.S. Air Force Thunderbirds

The New York Air Show is held each Memorial Day weekend. During the two-day event, the U.S. Air Force Thunderbirds (*left*), the U.S. Army Golden Knights, and many other aerial acts perform death-defying maneuvers and pay homage to Long Island's contributions to the field of aeronautics.

ROBERT MOSES

FOREVER ALTERING THE landscape of one of the world's greatest cities doesn't happen without ruffling a few feathers. Just ask master builder Robert Moses, one of the most polarizing figures in the history of urban planning.

Moses wasn't known as a man of heart (when he died of heart disease in 1981, some joked it was proof that he actually had one). However, it was his vision of an urban landscape dominated by highways and cars that helped enable the development of the suburbs. On Long Island, Moses was responsible for both the Northern and Southern state parkways, thoroughfares linking New York City to the 'burbs. The project was met with overwhelming opposition, especially from wealthy New Yorkers living on the island who shuddered at the idea of an influx of the "rabble."

A few years later, Moses designed Jones Beach, his first great achievement as chairman of the State Council of Parks. The extravagant park was met with overwhelming success.

Over the course of his life, Moses built a total of 658 parks, 416 miles of parkways, and 13 bridges.

Jones Beach features two ornate bathhouses, East and West. Built in 1931, the West Bath House stands adjacent to the boardwalk and is within walking distance of the shoreline.

On a hot summer day, the biggest challenge at Jones Beach is finding a spot on the sand close to the surf. The ocean breezes and waves draw thousands of visitors to the site each day.

FIRE ISLAND

Fire Island's documented history goes back to 1653 when Babylon's Isaac Stratford built a whaling station called Whalehouse Point. During its early years, Fire Island was known by shippers as the dangerous southernmost outpost of Long Island, located just off the mainland.

By the late 1700s and into the 1800s, Fire Island built a reputation as both an area patrolled by pirates and one that caused many shipwrecks. In fact, hundreds of ships were reported in distress in the early 1800s off Fire Island, prompting the construction of its first lighthouse in 1825. That lighthouse was replaced in 1858, and today's Fire Island Lighthouse is 168 feet from bottom to top (156 steps), making it the tallest in New York. It can be seen from more than 20 miles away.

Fire Island's history as a beach resort can be traced to 1855, when David Sammis arrived and established the Surf Hotel in the area now known as Kismet. The hotel operated for more than 30 years, and the area became New York's first state park in 1908.

After the turn of the century, Fire Island grew as beach houses began sprouting in the newly founded communities of Ocean Beach and Saltaire. Cherry Grove and Fire Island Pines were established later and became popular with the gay community. While there are less than 500 year-round residents on Fire Island, that number swells to hundreds of thousands of extended-stay visitors and day-trippers during the summer.

Long Island's Great Hurricane of 1938 caused havoc on Fire Island and knocked down many of the summer homes. However, residents rebuilt the area and banded together to keep it free of vehicles and overdevelopment. Today, most of the 31-mile-long Fire Island remains restricted to automobiles, forcing visitors to arrive by private boat or via the many South Shore ferries that service the area.

Fire Island's close proximity to the Atlantic Ocean proved fatal as many of the area's summer homes were severely damaged or destroyed during the Great Hurricane of 1938.

Fire Island Lighthouse

The Fire Island Lighthouse was lit for the first time on November 1, 1858. The 168-foot-tall tower cost $40,000 to construct, and its original four wicks were lit with fuel until 1938. Today, the working lighthouse and its museum are a popular tourist destination at the Fire Island National Seashore. For the brave at heart, the view from the exterior catwalk is one of the best on Long Island.

Travelers can reach Fire Island via one of the ferries that run from Bay Shore, Patchogue, or Sayville. The riders at left were lucky enough to catch a Great South Bay sunset on their return trip to Long Island.

TWA Flight 800 International Memorial

The TWA Flight 800 Memorial was built in 2004 on a two-acre parcel at Smith Point Park in Shirley. The memorial is situated near the last piece of land the flight crossed before it crashed into the Atlantic Ocean in 1996, killing all 230 people on board. The memorial was funded by the families of the victims and includes 14 flags, representing the homelands of the victims.

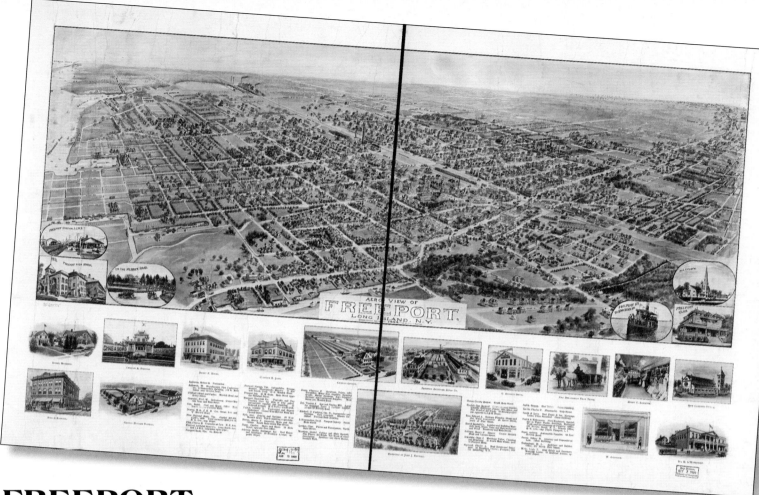

This 1909 overhead view of the Freeport community highlights its status as one of the bustling centers of Long Island during the early 20th century.

FREEPORT

Freeport's name is derived from its seafaring past. During the 1800s, when ship captains would arrive at what was once called Raynortown, they could land their cargo without customs dues—hence "Free Port."

In 1868, the railroad came and heralded a development boom. John Randall, who dredged several canals that run through the community, led the way; by 1902, Freeport ran trolleys to Brooklyn and Queens, bringing city dwellers to a dock where they could be ferried to the ocean beaches at Point Lookout.

During prohibition, the area was a center for clandestine rum running. The Freeport Point Shipyard ironically built both the rum-running boats and many of the Coast Guard cutters that chased them. The Columbian Bronze Company of Freeport built the propeller for the USS *Nautilus* submarine, a nuclear

sub that was the first to complete a submerged trek across the North Pole.

Freeport's former municipal stadium was an area attraction from 1931 to the 1980s, hosting stock car races and the Brooklyn Dodgers football team—yes, football—in the 1940s.

Bandleader Guy Lombardo called Freeport home for many years. "Mr. Freeport" Lombardo was a gold cup boating champion in 1946 and owned the popular East Point House restaurant.

Freeport is now probably best known for its Nautical Mile, an area along the Woodcleft Canal that was constructed to honor the community's seafaring past. Casino, fishing, and party boats travel the area's canals.

Tens of thousands of residents and visitors travel the boardwalk leading to Freeport's Nautical Mile. This stretch of shops, restaurants, and marinas is a tribute to Long Island's nautical history.

The Woodcleft Canal in Freeport is home to an assortment of boats, from leisure (such as the one on the left, shown in 1955) to salvage (*bottom left*).

GUY LOMBARDO'S EAST POINT HOUSE
FREEPORT, LONG ISLAND

Guy Lombardo

Bandleader Guy Lombardo was one of Freeport's most famous residents. His East Point House restaurant (*above*) was located at the south end of South Grove Street, which is now Guy Lombardo Avenue.

LONG BEACH

In the southwestern corner of Nassau County sits Long Beach, one of only two cities on Long Island. Developer Austin Corbin took the first shot at making a splash in Long Beach by partnering with the Long Island Rail Road in 1880. Shortly after, Corbin's company opened the Long Beach Hotel, a series of 27 cottages covering a 1,100-foot-stretch of beachfront. The hotel—then known as the world's largest—stood until 1907 when it burned down in an electrical fire.

In 1906, William Reynolds—politician, real estate developer, and public relations guru known for building amusement parks and hotels in Brooklyn—purchased most of Long Beach's oceanfront property. Reynolds's plan was to create the "Riviera of the East" by building hotels and homes in a Mediterranean, stucco style. This architecture is still prevalent in downtown Long Beach.

Reynolds had the channel on the north side of the beach dredged to allow steamships to bring more visitors to the area. (The aptly named Reynolds Channel remains today.) However, Reynolds couldn't stay out of the red and his company went bankrupt in 1918.

During the Roaring '20s and into the 1940s, celebrities flocked to Long Beach; Humphrey Bogart, James Cagney, and Rudolf Valentino all owned homes in the area. In 1939, tragedy struck Long Beach when Mayor Louis Edwards was assassinated by a city patrolman who felt he had been passed over for an important promotion.

After World War II, Long Beach fell on hard times. By the 1970s, the area was run down and facing an uncertain economic future. If not abandoned and boarded up, the once ornate hotels now held mental patients. However, an urban renewal effort in the early 1980s revitalized Long Beach to its past prominence.

This 1915 photo of the "Castle by the Sea" depicts the grandeur of strolling along the Long Beach boardwalk. The theater, built by developer William Reynolds, housed the world's largest dance floor.

The lavish Long Beach Hotel was built in 1880 by developer Austin Corbin, who called the hotel "the largest in the world." Unfortunately, an electrical fire in 1907 caused 800 guests to flee, severely injured eight people, and killed one woman.

After a time of economic and community despair, the Long Beach of today has been revitalized and refurbished. These oceanfront apartments and condominiums are sought after for their views and proximity to the community's famed boardwalk.

MARITIME MUSEUM

Long Island's Maritime Museum is nestled along the Great South Bay in West Sayville. A living testament to the region's seafaring history, the museum's exhibits revolve around the restoration of shipping vessels from years gone by. The work is carried out by a group of volunteers ranging from Eagle Scout candidates to senior citizens who all have one thing in common: a love of boats and the sea. Once the boats are restored they are either used as teaching tools or returned to their owners.

The 60-foot sloop *Priscilla* is the largest boat at the museum. Built in 1888, *Priscilla* sailed the waters of the Great South Bay and helped oystermen get their catch for almost 80 years. The dwindling supply of oysters and the boat's deteriorating wood hull forced its retirement and eventual donation to the museum.

The Maritime Museum also highlights the region's oystering past, shipwrecks and rescues, pirates, and historical diving equipment. The William Rudolph Oyster House was built in 1890 at the height of the region's oystering boom and is carefully preserved on-site to teach visitors how to shuck oysters. The Frank F. Penney boat shop arrived at the museum via the Great South Bay and serves as a working boathouse.

Today, the museum's boat basin serves the dual purpose of housing boats and providing a proper maritime backdrop for festivals and events. Its most unique tradition is the Halloween Boat Burning, in which a donated boat is burned. This is loosely based on the Viking tradition of nautical burial. Visitors dress in costumes, sing songs of the sea, and revel in the region's nautical traditions.

The sloop *Priscilla* was originally built in 1888 and came to the Maritime Museum in 1976. It has been refurbished several times over the years. Today, it's a floating remembrance of the region's cherished maritime past.

The Frank F. Penney boat shop at the Long Island Maritime Museum in West Sayville has proven to be seaworthy itself. In 1978, it was floated down the Great South Bay from Moriches to reach its current site. Built in 1900, the shop is the center of the museum's boat-building and restoration projects.

The Long Island Maritime Museum was founded in 1966. Its main building served as the garage of the Meadowedge estate. The museum's mission is to preserve Long Island's maritime history and heritage for educational purposes.

BELLPORT VILLAGE

Founded by sea captains Thomas and John Bell in the early 1800s, Bellport (the village that bears their name) was designed by the brothers to be a seaport. What started as a dock built by the Bell boys quickly expanded into a thriving community, stocked with boaters, shipbuilders, and fishermen.

The bay was the original source of income for village residents who fished, clammed, and oystered in its waters. Incorporated in 1910, the quaint South Shore village is also renowned for its Greek Revival and Victorian architecture, lending Bellport a distinctly New England feel.

The community's historic district is one of the largest on Long Island and features more than 80 homes listed on the National Register of Historic Places. Bellport's past is displayed at a two-acre historic campus in the heart of the village. Run by the historical society, the Museum Complex consists of preserved 19th-century buildings, including a milk house, art studio, gazebo, and a boathouse that features the restored Gil Smith catboat *Jealousy* and the *Three-in-One*, a fully rigged scooter.

In 1918, visiting author E. B. White wrote poetry about the idyllic village; former East End resident and future first lady Jacqueline Bouvier also summered in Bellport.

The village still runs a ferry from its coast out to the South Shore beaches. Bellport's theater, The Gateway Playhouse, features summer stock productions that draw numerous fledgling actors to the community. The playhouse's history dates back to 1941 when the property consisted of a mansion designed by Stanford White. Academy Award winner Robert Duvall is one of many famous alumni to pass through Gateway's program.

The Village of Bellport, located along the South Shore of Suffolk County, contains one of Long Island's largest historic districts. More than 80 homes are listed on the National Register of Historic Places. Its downtown shopping district (*below*) features many quaint shops that are a draw for local residents and regional visitors.

This Flower and Sons Company oyster boat patrols the waters off Long Island. However, the amount of oystering still going on in local waters has dwindled due to over-harvesting, tidal forces, and pollution. The house in the background once belonged to Billy Joel, a longtime Long Island resident.

OYSTERS

Oystering became popular on Long Island around 1850 when Dutch settlers came to the region to harvest the waters. The "Oyster King" of Long Island was Jacob Ockers, who set up the first major oyster processing plant in 1876.

Back then, a worker would shuck an average of 5,000 oysters per day. The Blue Point oyster, named for the community in which they were harvested and processed, became a delicacy and were featured at the finest restaurants in New York City, London, and Paris. They were served at the queen of England's table; her majesty only requested that the help sand down the shells because they were too rough.

Between 1890 and 1910, when dining out became more and more fashionable, more than two million bushels of oysters were harvested annually from Long Island waters. At the height of oyster mania there were more than 850 bars, saloons, and restaurants serving oysters, and more than 1,000 pushcarts selling the half-shell treat on street corners.

While
the Great Depression brought 25 percent unemployment to the entire country, the Long Island oyster companies were placing advertisements seeking thousands of shuckers and support staff. The end of the oyster boom started in the mid-1930s when over-harvesting and

disease hit the underwater oyster beds. Blue Points Oyster Company went under because, well, it went under. The Great Hurricane of 1938 caused 40-foot tidal surges and such a powerful underwater churn that the oyster beds were suffocated.

Although efforts to bring back the Long Island oyster continue, the industry has never recovered. Blue Points still harvests oysters along the South Shore, but it employs only 30 people—a far cry from the 1,000 on staff back in the day. Now oysters are grown in hatcheries and placed in waters along the coast of Mattituck on Long Island's North Fork.

In the late 1800s, oysters from Long Island were incredibly popular and abundant. The Blue Points Oyster Company (*below*, 1925) was one of the largest of the harvesters. Around the turn of the century, a worker could shuck in excess of 5,000 oysters per day; and as shown at left, Long Islanders know there's nothing tastier than a freshly shucked oyster.

THE BLUEPOINTS
OYSTERS AND CLA

While the largest oyster companies on Long Island used oyster boats and dredgers to get their catch, this lone oystermen used his own personal tongs to find his catch on the bottom of the shallow Great South Bay. Many Long Islanders made their livings in the late 1800s and early 1900s thanks to the rich and abundant oyster and clam beds.

CLAMMING

WHILE OYSTERS WERE ONCE the overwhelming food of choice in the region, don't discount the Long Island clam. For many years during the early to mid-1900s, hundreds of clamming boats patrolled the waters of the Great South Bay. At one point, Long Island was responsible for 75 percent of all the clams consumed in the United States. Today, while the clamming industry is not nearly what it once was, the Doxsee Clam Company is still going strong. Doxsee started in Islip in 1865 and relocated to Point Lookout in 1933. The company continues to harvest clams with Bob Doxsee, a fifth-generation descendent of founder James Harvey Doxsee, at the helm.

Festival on the Half Shell

The annual Oyster Festival—held at Theodore Roosevelt Park—began in 1984 and is ran by the Oyster Bay Rotary Club. Over 200,000 people attend each year, making it the largest waterfront festival on the East Coast. Over the course of the Columbus Day weekend (when the event takes place), over 50,000 oysters are served on the half shell, and that's in addition the wide range of seafood offered by various festival vendors.

Since 1963, All-American Drive-In in Massapequa has been a Long Island staple. Locals claim that the burgers, fries, and shakes are second to none. The owners must be doing something right as the crowds regularly wait out the door to sample the eatery's products.

ALL-AMERICAN DRIVE-IN

When it comes to going back to a simpler and cheaper way of life on Long Island, people wax poetic about Massapequa's All-American Drive-In, located on Merrick Road. All-American Drive-In opened in 1963 and remains a Long Island classic. Under continuous operation by the Vultaggio family since its inception, All-American is the place to hit for the best hamburger around. The french fries are hand-cut, and the vintage stand's franks and shakes are a blast from the greasy past.

Throughout the years, the facility's exterior hasn't changed much. And it's interior restaurant? Well, there is no interior

restaurant. Though times have certainly reshaped the classic burger joint of yesteryear, All-American is still a drive-in. The lines can be frighteningly long, especially on the weekends when high schoolers, college students, and families young and old flock to the eatery. But that's all part of the experience. Not to fret though—the Vultaggios and their staff have the ordering system down to a science, filling bellies with their renowned burgers quickly and efficiently. There are a few outside tables and benches, but most people either eat in their vehicles or take the burgers on their way, just like they did almost 50 years ago.

PIRATES

Long Island's famous shorelines and numerous ports have a history linked to the sea. Centuries ago, the sea was synonymous with the transportation of goods—precious, valuable goods. Long Island was a port of regular ingress and egress, making it a target for pirates who patrolled the waters looking for loot and easy prey.

The most famous of these pirates was the legendary William (Captain) Kidd. In 1699, he buried a small treasure on Gardiner's Island in a spot known as Cherry Grove Field (a bronze marker set into a stone marks the spot). The treasure was dug up and sent to England as evidence against Kidd and his pirating ways.

In 1728, a crew of 80 French and Spanish pirates overran Gardiner's Island, injuring several members of the Gardiner family. The pirates were furious that much of Gardiner's wealth was safe in East Hampton, but they still got away with most of the family silver.

Before and during the Revolutionary War, pirates patrolled many of the ports on Long Island's North Shore, trying to disrupt the naval supply chain of the British. Many methods were used, including late-night hijackings, capturing crews and captains, or sneak attacks to steal boats.

While pirating remained a constant throughout the 1800s, a new type of pirate reinvented the illegal swindling during Prohibition: the rumrunner. From 1920 through the mid-1930s, boats from Canada and the West Indies would anchor 12 miles off shore and sell liquor to men in speedboats, who would then race the purchase to shore. Waiting there would be a car, usually with an armed guard, that drove the liquor to the city for sale at the many speakeasies around town.

Legend has it that the famed swashbuckler Captain Kidd buried treasure on Gardiner's Island. The treasure was used in his trial—the outcome of which led to Kidd being hanged.

Long Island Pirate Festival

Long Island's Maritime Museum in West Sayville regularly pays homage to the region's pirating past. Each summer, actors show thousands of visitors what the buccaneer's life was really like through educational programs and reenactments.

Captain William Kidd's "Cloth of Gold" was presented to Mrs. John Gardiner on Gardiner's Island in June 1699. The cloth is made of metallic gold, silver thread, silk, and cotton. Today, it is part of the Long Island collection at the East Hampton Library.

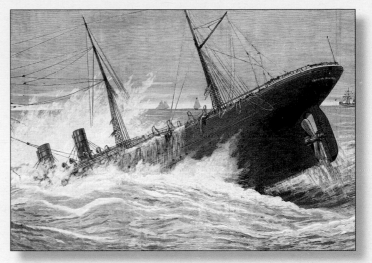

SHIPWRECKS

THROUGHOUT ITS SEAFARING HISTORY, the waters off the North and South shores of Long Island have claimed hundreds of ships, giving the region the ominous nickname "Wreck Valley." One of the most horrific wrecks took place on January 13, 1840, off the coast of the Long Island Sound.

The steamboat *Lexington* caught fire soon after departing New York for Connecticut. Cotton bales were placed too close to the ship's boiler, which started a fire that spread rapidly. Only four people survived the tragedy; 139 perished. Today, the Lexington wreck is buried under 140 feet of water in the Long Island Sound.

On March 14, 1886, the USS *Oregon* collided with a schooner just off the Fire Island coast. All the passengers on the schooner perished, though the eight hours the *Oregon* stayed afloat allowed enough time for all 845 passengers and crew to be saved.

There are scores of stories of whaling boats, ships engaged in battles during the War of 1812, and other passenger ships and freighters who all visited Davy Jones's Locker off Long Island's shores. Long Island's history with life-saving stations and the U.S. Coast Guard can all be attributed to the many shipwrecks that have happened over the years.

BRIGHTWATERS

The Village of Brightwaters has its roots firmly planted in the vision of the Ackerson brothers: Thomas B., Charles, Henry, and Pierre. In 1907, the quintet purchased 1,200 acres of land in west Bay Shore to create their idea of a model community. It took eight years and caused the Ackerson Company to collapse financially, but their community has stood the test of time—Brightwaters is one of Long Island's most beautiful and sought-after places to live.

The Ackersons' original property was swampland. They transformed this land into a "Venetian Yacht Harbor" that was 175 feet wide, 20 feet deep, and just short of a mile long. Today, their boat landing holds hundreds of boats. Its ornate early 20th-century architecture remains one of the most unique outdoor areas in the region, and the homes built around the harbor match the area's splendor.

The brothers also preserved space for public beaches. Other land that was set aside has since become two pristine parks: Wohseepee and George Walker Memorial Park on the Bay.

Brightwaters residents banded together and incorporated as a village in 1916. Shortly after, Thomas B. Ackerson paved the way for the creation of a boat canal and park. He served as the first village leader.

Today, the village is incredibly well manicured and most of the homes are within close proximity to one of the five lakes, the canal, or the Great South Bay. Just as the Ackersons originally envisioned, Brightwaters remains a quiet and quaint South Shore community.

Main Street in Bay Shore during the early 1900s was a bustling area filled with retail and living space. This building on the corner of Bay Shore Road and Main Street contained a brick garage in the rear, two large double stores, and three 5-room apartments.

In the foreground of the gazebo at Babylon's Argyle Park stands this monument to veterans of World War II, the Korean War, and the Vietnam War who paid the ultimate price in service to their country. The canals of Bay Shore and Brightwaters (*right*) were built in the late 1800s and early 1900s to provide boaters easy access to their homes and yards. Today, this type of waterfront property is much sought-after on the South Shore of Suffolk County.

This crime scene photo shows the home at 112 Ocean Avenue in Amity Harbor where Ronald DeFeo Jr. killed six members of his family in 1974. The brutal crime inspired the book (and eventual movie) *The Amityville Horror*.

AMITYVILLE HORROR

One of the country's most famous haunted homes, a picturesque, six-bedroom Dutch Colonial, still stands in Amity Harbor. The home, located at 112 Ocean Avenue, features an inviting porch and a boathouse. If it weren't for tales of the "Amityville Horror"—which has spawned a series of books and movies—it would be your typical coastal Long Island homestead.

In 1975, George and Kathy Lutz bought the home for the bargain price of $80,000. Along with their three children, the couple moved in and even inherited some of the previous owner's furnishings. There was just one glitch in the deal: A little more than a year prior, the unassuming home was the site of a multiple homicide—it was where Ronald DeFeo Jr. murdered six members of his own family.

What followed next has found its way into the public consciousness through at least ten books and nine different movies.

The Lutzs' stories of horrific and paranormal activities at the home, including seeing oozing walls and hearing terrifying sounds, were documented by author Jay Anson in the 1977 best seller *The Amityville Horror—A True Story*. The first movie, starring James Brolin and Margot Kidder, was released in 1979 and was a huge hit, causing the home's reputation to burgeon.

The Lutzs' time at the house lasted only 28 days; they fled, fearing for their safety. Through the years there have been several other owners of the home, none of whom experienced the same paranormal activities reported by the Lutz family.

To the dismay of many local property owners, the home still manages to draw plenty of car and foot traffic from ghoulish curiosity seekers.

The Amityville Horror house today is an updated Dutch Colonial that fits right into the affluent community where it was built. Much to the chagrin of the neighbors, the home still attracts lots of traffic from horror fans.

Amityville Horror

Jay Anson's 1977 book highlighted the alleged horrific events within the famed Amity Harbor home and became a national best seller. In 1979, it was followed by a hugely successful movie starring James Brolin and Margot Kidder (*right*). Several less successful sequels were made, taking the alleged facts of the case into the realm of extreme supernatural fiction.

Living off the Land and Sea

The North Fork is unlike any other community on Long Island. Native Americans were the first to farm the fertile soil and were usurped by the early English and Dutch settlers. The newcomers marveled at how much better the soil was in comparison to their native Europe. Although farming remains a staple today, land has become more scarce and more valuable to develop.

Long Island was still a land of crops in the mid-20th century; 72,000 acres of potatoes were farmed in Nassau and Suffolk in 1945, with much of that coming from the North Fork. And while the North Fork still produces fine crops of potatoes, beets, lettuce, and other fruits and vegetables, a new industry was spawned in 1973.

WINE COUNTRY

The beginning of the North Fork's shift from farmland to wine country came in 1973. That year, Alex and Louise Hargrave planted the area's first vineyard. Since then, the region has grown from its humble beginnings of one vineyard (and the opening of the Hargrave winery in 1975) to its current offering of more than 30 wineries featuring wine tastings, music festivals, hay rides, and tours of the facilities. In a little more than 35 years, "the enchanted East End of Long Island has become one of the world's great vineyard regions," explains David Rosengarten, Food Network personality and cookbook author.

The growth of wine country, which now features 3,000 acres of vineyards, has also changed the complexion of the North Fork: More than 1.2 million visitors came to the region in 2008 specifically for the wine.

ORIENT POINT

While wine country may be a great attraction for visitors to the East End of Long Island's North Fork, the area is filled with a rich seafaring history as well. Orient Point is the North Fork's eastern-

The Great Hurricane of 1938 struck the East End of Long Island at 3:30 P.M. on September 21 with sustained winds of more than 120 mph. In its wake, the hurricane took more than 50 lives on Long Island and caused millions of dollars in damage to homes, boats, and the environment. This photo shows a fish market at the foot of Main Street in Southold just after the hurricane made landfall.

In the early 1900s, the Greenport Opera House hosted many productions. Its location on Front Street, which also used to house a post office and store, was demolished in 1936 and replaced with a movie theater.

The potato was the staple crop of Long Island through the late 1940s, especially on the North Fork where the fertile soil drew farmers from throughout Europe. Though the crop has dwindled in recent years, potatoes are still harvested on Long Island, as evidenced by this 2006 photo.

most point and dates its development to before the Revolutionary War, back to when British General Benedict Arnold ran meetings in local taverns during the 1770s. Orient Point is home to the Bug Light, a lighthouse nicknamed as such because of its squat shape; its position in Orient Harbor has alerted boaters to the impending coastline since its construction in 1871.

SAFE PASSAGE

Located just west of Orient Point is historic Greenport, the region's largest community. Greenport's history dates back to 1682 as a coastal town with strong ties to New England. Since there was no way off of Long Island other than by boat until the opening of the Brooklyn Bridge in 1883, Greenport's location provided travelers with a relatively quick passage to coastal Connecticut, Rhode Island, and Massachusetts.

This popular port community brought many shipbuilding establishments to the area. From the early 19th century through World War II, more than 550 ships were built and launched in Greenport. Greenport is also known as the home of Captain George Monsell. Monsell sailed his team, the majestic J's, to victory in the America's Cup in 1930, 1934, and 1937.

The Long Island Rail Road's eastern-most terminus had its golden spike hammered into the Greenport track in 1844, allowing people to travel in from Brooklyn, Queens, and other points west. Greenport's strong ties to the railroad are memorialized at the current Railroad Museum of Long Island, which has preserved many original structures and trains.

Today, Greenport remains a popular destination for history buffs looking to ride the antique carousel in the village green or visit the Jail & Police Museum. After a long day of sightseeing, fresh seafood can be enjoyed at one of the many downtown eateries, some of which date back to the turn of the 20th century.

GIMME SHELTER

Between Long Island's two eastern forks sits historic Shelter Island. Accessible only by boat, the island offers ferries running from Greenport and the South Fork. Shelter Island's ferry service dates back to 1893 when the *Menantic*, the first double-sided ferry ever built,

brought people to and from the island. Today, travelers are able to haul their cars to the island utilizing much more modern ferries.

Shelter Island is also known for its beautiful and historic architecture. Shelter Island Heights was envisioned and built as a planned community by Robert Morris Copeland in the late 1800s. Union Chapel, the visual and social center of Copeland's plan, was built in 1875 and was placed on the national register of historic places in 1984. It is the oldest public building on the island. There are many other historic buildings preserved on Shelter Island, including Havens House, where George Washington once slept in the late 1700s.

SOUTHOLD

A little farther west on the North Fork rests Southold, Long Island's first English settlement (circa 1640). Southold was settled by English Puritans from New Haven and remained aligned with New Haven until 1662 and Connecticut until 1674. Today, the community is made up of a historic shopping district and architecture that remains true to its English roots.

An eclectic mix of farming communities and farm stands, modern wineries, and 300-year-old barns and buildings remain throughout the North Fork—all standing as a testament to the region's unique evolution as one of the country's first settled areas.

The main crops on the North Fork today are wine grapes. More than 30 wineries and 60 vineyards have sprouted since the 1970s, drawing positive reviews and millions of tourist dollars to the region.

ORIENT POINT

During the American Revolution, Benedict Arnold and a group of British commanders and local Tories set up a base of operations at Orient Point to launch attacks against Connecticut. Today, tens of thousands of travelers take the Cross Sound Ferry from Orient Point to New London, Connecticut—the echoes of war long silenced. The ferry riders utilize the crossing to trek to nearby Connecticut casinos or for a faster route to Providence, Boston, or other New England locales.

Because it is so remote, Orient Point has just over 500 year-round residents; its diminutive downtown area features only a post office and a few small shops, yet thousands of visitors still come to the community each year.

The waters off Orient Point are home to two of Long Island's most creatively named lighthouses. The Coffee Pot stands 64 feet high and was constructed in 1899. It takes its name from the thickness of its base. In 1970, the U.S. Coast Guard attempted to shut it down, but community opposition led to its refurbishing. The Pot remains a functioning lighthouse.

Also located just off Orient Point is the Bug Light, a 63-foot-high lighthouse built in 1871. The Bug Light has a unique two-story building attached to its base that serves as the home of the lightkeeper. Over the years, the Bug faced many obstacles to its survival, including having its foundation completely replaced in 1924. In 1963, vandals entered the lighthouse and burned it down. However, the lighthouse was rebuilt in 1990 and is fully operational today.

Plum Island

The Plum Island Animal Disease Research Center opened in 1954 off the coast of the North Fork and has long been a source of controversy. The lab, which has been shrouded in secrecy since its inception, began as an animal disease facility, but its focus eventually switched to biological warfare research. Since then, deadly viruses have been released into the air on two separate occasions. Some speculate that the West Nile virus was introduced to the United States via Plum Island. In 2003, the Department of Homeland Security took control of the safety and security of the island. The cattle chute for Lab 257 (*above*) was shut down in 1995.

Sailing has long been popular off the waters of the North Fork. The *Rainbow,* seen above, won the America's Cup in 1934 for Captain George Monsell of Greenport. Monsell and his crew, the majestic J's, also won the Cup in 1930 and in 1937.

The Greenport Basin and Construction Company began operations in the 19th century and grew to become one of the area's largest boatbuilders. Above, its boat the *Mascot* is readied for launch in 1906.

GREENPORT

From its earliest settlements, Greenport has been tied to the sea. Its proximity to the easternmost point of the North Fork has provided easy passage to New England and has led its residents to pursue jobs in whaling, fishing, and shipbuilding.

East End whalers were drawn to Greenport's coastal locale; the first-known whaling boat was the *Petosi,* which was christened in 1830. Greenport's most famous resident of the time, David Gelston Floyd (grandson of William Floyd, Long Island's only signer of the Declaration of Independence), operated a fleet of whaling boats. The industry proved quite profitable for Floyd, who constructed Brecknock Hall in 1857. At the time, it was considered one of the most beautiful homes on Long Island. After years of use, the house fell into disre-

pair and was abandoned. In 2004, a volunteer foundation was formed; workers dedicated more than 19,000 hours to restoring the estate.

As more people were drawn to Greenport in the mid-1850s, shipbuilding became the primary employer and the biggest industry. In total, six shipbuilding companies existed in the community.

During World War I, the Greenport Basin and Construction Company was the region's largest shipbuilder; it made its mark constructing torpedo boats for the U.S. Navy. In World War II, it became the East End's largest employer, providing work on wartime vessels. The company still operates in Greenport, now as Greenport Yacht and Ship Building Company.

An aerial view of Greenport shows off its relationship to the sea. The reason for its name is clear by the lush fields located throughout the region.

Downtown Greenport

The Greenport Jail & Police Museum (*below*) features memorabilia and other historic items. The original jail was built in 1917. Not far is the Maritime Museum (*left*), which features a collection of rare Fresnal lenses.

Greenport's downtown marina remains a draw for boaters from across the eastern seaboard. They can dock downtown, enjoy a meal, shop, and have easy access to marine supplies.

WINE COUNTRY

Long Island's wine country was born along the North Fork in Cutchogue in 1973 when Alex and Louisa Hargrave planted the region's first vineyard. Even though they sold their vineyard in 1999, the Hargraves started a new and thriving industry with unparalleled growth.

The wine region has grown to become Long Island's largest tourist attraction, featuring more than 50 producers and 60 vineyards. Spread over 3,000 acres, the vineyards produce about 500,000 cases per vintage. Today, the vast majority of Long Island's winemakers are located on the North Fork, and most of the wineries feature tours, tastings, and outdoor events.

With the Long Island Sound to the north and the Atlantic Ocean to the south, the region's temperate coastal climate is perfect for growing grapes and reminds some vintners of France. The former bumper crop on the North Fork used to be the Long Island potato, but the vineyards have replaced many of the potato farms. A few wineries, in fact, are even built into old potato barns.

Some aficionados consider Long Island to be a "young" area for producing wine, though many of the vineyards have received national and international awards and accolades. New York is the fourth largest wine producer in the country, behind California, Washington, and Oregon, and the influx of Long Island products has strengthened the state's national standing.

While Long Island wines are shipped across the country and overseas, the bulk of its product goes to supplying merchants and restaurants on both Long Island and in New York City.

This scene at the Martha Clara Vineyards tasting room in Riverhead is a common one throughout Long Island's North Fork each summer and autumn.

The Hargrave Vineyard in Cutchogue is Long Island's first vineyard. It was originally planted in 1973. Shown here are its cabernet sauvignon grapes growing on the vine.

This villa may look like it's located in France, but this traditional wine country scene is actually from the Lenz Winery in Peconic.

SHELTER ISLAND

In 1652, Nathaniel Sylvester, a sugar merchant from Barbados, had the first-known structure on Shelter Island built for his 16-year-old wife (it was completed before they arrived). Though rebuilt by descendants in 1733, "Sylvester Manor" still stands on the island today. The Sylvester family brought others to the Shelter Island community in the early 1700s; they became known for giving refuge to persecuted Quakers from surrounding areas—hence the name.

Shelter Island is renowned for its folk architecture, especially in Shelter Island Heights, one of the country's first planned communities. In 1871, a group of Brooklyn clergymen created the Shelter Island Grove and built several summer resorts that draw thousands of visitors each year.

Early development reflects the vision of architect Frederick Law Olmsted—the designer of New York's Central Park—and Robert Morris Copeland. Copeland designed many homes in the Shelter Island Heights area, building 70 cottages between 1872 and 1880. These homes were centered around Union Chapel, another Copeland creation, which was built in 1875. The Heights area, where many of these homes still stand, was listed in the National Register of Historic Places in 1993; Union Chapel received the same distinction in 1984.

In 1893, the first double-sided ferry ever built, the *Menantic*, took passengers from Greenport to Shelter Island. That ferry line still operates today. Shelter Island is also home to Dering Harbor, the smallest community in New York, with a population of 13.

Today, thanks to a committed historical society, Shelter Island's architectural and Colonial history have been richly preserved; hundreds of well-maintained structures from the 18th and 19th centuries continue to dot the bucolic landscape.

The Havens House

William Havens built the home above in 1743 on Shelter Island. His son, James, inherited the home but was best known as a member of the Provincial Congress in 1775–76.

Prospect House

This hotel in Shelter Island Heights was built in 1872 as a place for summer tourists. The Prospect House was a popular vacation spot until it burned down in 1923. It was rebuilt, but burned down again in 1942. Today, the land where it stood is used as a town park.

Reachable only by ferry, Shelter Island remains a popular and secluded summer vacation spot. Its charming architecture and elevation changes are evident throughout the island.

GARDINER'S ISLAND

Located between Long Island's two forks, the history of Gardiner's Island goes back to 1639 when Lion Gardiner first settled there. He reportedly bought the island from Chief Wyandanch of the Montaukett Native Americans for a few items, including a dog, some blankets, and gunpowder. In 1989, the island was valued at $125 million, making it one of the greatest land purchases since the Dutch bought Manhattan.

The island has remained in the Gardiner family's hands for almost 400 years. It's one of the oldest and largest family-owned islands in the world and is the only remaining real estate in the country that was purchased with a royal grant from the English Crown.

During the American Revolution, the British regularly entered the island to take and destroy crops. In 1820, Julia Gardiner, eventual wife to President John Tyler, was born on the island. By the mid-1930s, the high cost of the island's upkeep forced its sale. Sara Gardiner purchased it for $400,000, keeping it in the family.

In 1953, after Sara's death, the island was passed to her nephew Robert Lion Gardiner. Although considered eccentric, he remained the 13th "Lord of the Manor" for many years. Robert Lion Gardiner had no children of his own, so the island passed down to his great niece, Alexandra Goelet.

Today, Gardiner's Island remains one of the most pristine places in the United States. The island, which is six miles long and three miles wide, features the largest stand of white oak trees in the Northeast. The island also has the biggest population of ospreys in the state; the birds have no natural predators on the island, enabling their unique practice of building nests along the ground.

The Gardiner's Island Windmill was built in 1795 and added to the National Register of Historic Places in 1978. With its brilliant white paint job and proximity to the shoreline, boaters traveling past the island can't miss this windmill.

Julia Gardiner was the first lady of the United States and the wife of U.S. President John Tyler.

This Gardiner Manor house was built in 1774 by David Gardiner, the sixth proprietor of Gardiner's Island.

The Prince Building on Main Road in Southold was built in 1874 as a dry goods store. The photo at right was taken circa 1890. Today, the building has been completely restored and serves as the headquarters of the Southold Historical Society.

SOUTHOLD

Founded by Puritans from New Haven in 1640, Southold is considered the oldest English settlement in New York. The Puritans, led by Reverend John Youngs, left Connecticut to escape religious persecution and built their church in the new community.

By the American Revolution, Southold had grown into an agricultural community—one that was overtaken by British troops. Many of the people were loyal to the British, while the Yankees fled to nearby Connecticut. After the British left, life in the area was difficult for Southold residents who had little means—other than farming—to make a living. But when the railroad came to the North Fork in 1844, that all changed. The rail system enabled residents to send their produce west, thus increasing their prosperity.

Because of its coastal setting, Southold became a popular place with tourists from New York City and other points west. Some of these summer visitors decided to build second homes in the community, leading to its inception as a vacation haven. Rooming houses and hotels popped up in downtown Southold, the largest of which was the Southold Hotel, built in 1830 and demolished in 1920. Some pieces of the old hotel were built into homes in downtown Southold.

Historic Southold

Southold is one of Long Island's most picturesque and historic communities. Founded in 1640, the First Presbyterian Church (*left*) has stood on its current site since 1803. Markers in its graveyard, some of which were shipped from England, date back to 1672. The Ann-Currie Bell House (*above*) was constructed around 1900 and provides a fine example of late Victorian architecture. Today, the home is part of the Southold Historical Society and Museum's Maple Lane Complex, which contains 12 different historic structures.

Custer Institute

Stargazers enjoy Long Island's Custer Institute and Observatory on Main Bayview Road in Southold. Founded in 1927, it is the oldest public observatory of its kind in the region, and every Saturday, from dusk until midnight, institute volunteers guide the public to see the stars through the many telescopes housed at the facility. Charles W. Elmer, founder of the Perkin-Elmer Optical Company and an avid amateur astronomer, originally founded the institute. The current structure opened in 1938 and has been updated and expanded since. The institute gets its name from Elmer's wife, whose maiden name was Custer (and who was the grand niece of General George Armstrong Custer).

Horton Point

Horton Point Lighthouse (*left*) has sat majestically as a beacon to boaters at the northern tip of Southold since 1857. Originally commissioned by the U.S. Lighthouse Service, Horton Point is one of seven lighthouses in Southold. The lighthouse was home to ten different keepers from 1857 until 1933, the year the lighthouse became automated. Today, part of the keeper's former residence is used as a nautical museum. The large rocks located on the shore of the Long Island Sound (*above*) remain a popular place for anglers to try their luck.

FARMING CULTURE

Long Island's fertile soil and temperate climate have always drawn farmers to the region. One of Long Island's most popular and valuable products through the years has been the potato, though the region is not as recognized as Idaho.

In 1866, there were 275,000 acres of potato crops in New York; estimates placed half of them on Long Island. Beginning in the early 19th century and continuing over the next 100 years, Irish and Polish immigrants dominated the East End farms. The East End saw its potato crops flourish as irrigation improved, machines for digging and planting were invented, and better plows were developed.

Near the turn of the century, the Long Island Rail Road began operating its "Farmer's Trains," which brought potatoes from the East End directly to New York City. Throughout the early 1900s, the potato remained a strong cash crop; 43,000 acres of potatoes were planted in 1933, and that number grew to 72,000 acres by 1945. But as suburban development took hold, potato farms were forced to move farther east. In 1979, there were still 50,000 acres of potato fields on Long Island; almost all of them were planted on the East End. Eventually, though, farmers found that selling their land was more profitable than planting new crops. By the turn of the 21st century, only 6,000 acres of potato fields remained.

In recent years, farmers and other business people have created successful products utilizing the Long Island potato. Martin Sidor Farms now makes North Fork Potato Chips, which are made from potatoes grown on a 170-acre potato farm in Mattituck; Long Island Spirits distills its LiV Vodka at an 80-acre former potato farm on Long Island's North Fork.

Long Island was key in feeding Allied troops during World War II. The total potato crop was valued at $30 million at the end of the war. Today, local potatoes grown on the East End are used to make North Fork Potato Chips, a popular regional snack.

Riverhead's Hallockville Museum Farm pays homage to the community's historic farming past. The campus contains 18 houses, barns, and outbuildings, the oldest being the Hallock family homestead, constructed in the mid-18th century. Visitors can tour the buildings, experience hands-on farming in the fields, or meet the facility's many farm animals.

Peconic Land Trust

The Peconic Land Trust is a nonprofit organization founded in 1983 by John Halsey to ensure the protection of Long Island's farms, heritage, and natural lands. As development has spread across Long Island, the trust has been able to protect more than 9,500 acres, mostly on Long Island's East End. Above, ospreys fly over a field of wetlands in their natural environment along the Hamptons coast.

MATTITUCK STRAWBERRY FESTIVAL

Who would have thought that honoring a locally grown fruit could have such appeal? Mattituck's annual Strawberry Festival, held each June, has become one of the North Fork's most popular events for ushering in the start of the summer season.

Since 1955, the Lions Club has hosted the festival just as the locally grown strawberries are reaching their peak ripeness and flavor. The idea started when three Mattituck Lions traveled to the Plant City Florida Festival in 1954; they returned to Long Island with the belief that Mattituck's strawberry crop would be perfect for an annual celebration. The event was born the following year. That first festival lasted three days and drew 1,000 people; today it attracts more than 40,000 people.

While the fest has expanded to include a number of foods, it remains centered around the strawberry, which can be sampled in shortcake, as jams and jellies, or covered in chocolate, among many other delicious creations. The festival has also grown to include hundreds of arts and craft vendors, amusements and rides, fireworks, farming demonstrations, and the crowning of the annual Strawberry Queen.

The Mattituck Lions still use the event as a way to raise funds for the many nonprofits they serve, just like they did in 1955.

One of the North Fork's most popular events is the Mattituck Strawberry Festival, which brings a true slice of old-time Americana to the region. Since 1955, the festival has paid homage to the region's vibrant strawberry crop. Visitors get to eat and drink strawberry products (such as the delectable chocolate-covered strawberries shown at top), go on rides, view and purchase arts and crafts, and watch flatbed trucks haul enormous, inflatable strawberries around town.

The South Fork: Playground of the Rich and Famous

About 25 years ago, a wise slogan writer dubbed Long Island's Montauk Point "The End." Not exactly groundbreaking, considering that Montauk is the last rocky strip of land (and the farthest point east) on Long Island. However, the slogan was creative and catchy enough to put on bumper stickers and T-shirts for locals and tourists alike.

As one of Long Island's best known communities, Montauk is more than just a slogan: It's the Montauk Lighthouse, rock fishing off the jetty, and some of the best ocean fishing around. Montauk's waters and anglers inspired one of America's most beloved movies, *Jaws*. The Captain Quint character is said to be modeled after Montauk's own shark-fishing curmudgeon, Frank Mundus.

Montauk's history goes back to some of the country's formative events. The Deep Hollow Ranch was founded in 1658 and is the country's oldest continually operating cattle ranch. The HMS *Culloden* ran aground off Montauk in 1781 while pursuing a French frigate; remains of the ship were found in the 1970s and the wreckage is now on the National Register of Historic Places as New York's only underwater park, drawing divers to explore its remains.

Another famous incident involving a ship on Montauk made it all the way to the silver screen. In 1839, slaves seized the schooner *La Amistad*; when the white crew led them to believe they had returned to Africa, the mutineers came ashore looking for food and supplies. Though the slaves were eventually

Area firefighters show off their prowess during a turn-of-the-century firefighter's contest held in Southampton. On the right is the Edward J. Fisher Restaurant and Bakery.

Since 1796, the Montauk Lighthouse has stood as a beacon to boaters and a symbol of Long Island's coastal geography at the easternmost point on Long Island.

This imposing figure is none other than author John Steinbeck (shown in 1962), who drew writing inspiration from the history, natural environment, and tranquility surrounding his Sag Harbor home.

captured, they were awarded their freedom after a sensational trial.

THE RICH AND FAMOUS
While Montauk may be dubbed "The End," the Hamptons are just the beginning of the land of milk and honey on Long Island's South Fork. From East Hampton through Bridgehampton and into Southampton, the area has been attracting the glitterati for decades.

Drawn by the peaceful waters, world-class beaches, luxurious homes, and close proximity to New York City, many A-list celebrities choose the Hamptons as a spot for summer homes. Residents include Spielberg, Streisand, McCartney, Alda, and Seinfeld.

Beyond the incredible wealth of its residents, the Hamptons also feature

some of the finest shopping along the main streets. Smack-dab in the middle of downtown Southampton's restaurants, art galleries, and designer boutiques rests Hildreth's department store. It has been the centerpiece of the downtown community since 1842, when it opened as a general store. Today, Hildreth's—which is still a family-run business—has grown to four East End locations and more than 80,000 total square feet of retail space.

More than 40,000 sports lovers flock to Bridgehampton each August for the Hampton Classic Horse Show, which has grown into one of the largest hunter/jumper shows in the country. The Classic has taken place on the South Fork throughout its 75-plus-year history.

The South Fork also boasts many examples of historic architecture, including a host of windmills, many of which still function. The Shinnecock Windmill—which was constructed in the 18th century—rests on top of a hill at Stony Brook Southampton College as the campus centerpiece. In East Hampton, the Old Hook Mill still stands on Montauk Highway; it celebrated its 200th birthday in 2006.

SHINNECOCK
The Hamptons also feature a rich history of Native American heritage. Southampton's Shinnecock Indian Nation is more than 200 years old and currently has more than 1,300 residents, 600 of whom still live on its Southampton reservation. Each fall the Shinnecock hold their

annual powwow to honor their culture and history.

The Shinnecock Golf Club is also located in Southampton. Built in 1891, the clubhouse is considered the oldest in the United States. In 1896, the second U.S. Open Golf Championship was contested on the course (with James Foulis as the victor). The Open has since been played at Shinnecock in 1986, 1995, and 2004.

PRESIDENTIAL TREATMENT
Northeast of Southampton rests Sag Harbor, one of Long Island's most historic and well-preserved communities. Sag Harbor is the home of President Chester A. Arthur's summer residence as well as the Umbrella House, which housed British Troops during the Revolutionary War and was struck by cannon fire during the War of 1812.

The easternmost point of the South Fork features areas such as Hampton Bays and Westhampton Beach; both are populated each summer by college students and young families who prefer the affordable housing and rental options.

From the eastern tip of Long Island through the glamour of the Hamptons and ending in the beach-side communities along the shore, the South Fork remains a popular area for vacationers, famous or otherwise. It's just the spot for anyone seeking a lazy day at the beach or an eye-catching sunset.

The Hook Mill, one of many windmills on Long Island's South Fork, has stood on a small mound on the East End of East Hampton since 1806. The mill, which is still operational, is open to the public from June to September.

Anglers come from near and far to test their luck casting off the rocks at Montauk Point. It's easy to understand how the sunny skies, blue ocean water, and marvelous backdrop can be such a draw. This photo, captured in 1939, could very well have been taken this summer as very little has changed at the foot of the lighthouse over the years.

MONTAUK POINT

The journey to the top of the 110-foot-tall Montauk Lighthouse is the same now as it was when it opened back in 1796. Though it's a haul up the 137 steps and around the winding, narrow tower leading to the top, the reward—a panoramic view of Rhode Island, Connecticut, and the Atlantic—is worth it. Construction on the lighthouse was authorized in 1792, making it the oldest in New York. Its beacon still flashes every five seconds and can be seen as far away as 19 nautical miles.

Just west of the lighthouse is Montauk's Deep Hollow Ranch. Opened in 1658, it is the country's oldest operational cattle ranch. Deep Hollow housed 6,000 heads of cattle at its summit in the 1770s and is dubbed the "Birthplace of the American Cowboy."

Montauk has also enjoyed a rich seafaring history. In 1781, the British HMS *Culloden* ran aground off Montauk while pursuing a French frigate; its remains weren't discovered until the 1970s and have since been converted into the only underwater park in New York.

Whale watching, alongside deep-sea fishing, is entwined in both Montauk's past and present. Montauk's most famous angler is Frank Mundus, who hunted shark for decades during the early 20th century. The Robert Shaw character from *Jaws* was reportedly based on Mundus's life.

The Great Hurricane of 1938 devastated Montauk. The storm leveled the downtown shopping district, toppled homes, and wreaked havoc on the fishing industry. The community rebuilt, however, and remains strong today.

Today, Montauk's Lighthouse still flashes its light every five seconds. Visitors can traverse the 137 steps to the top of its 110-foot tower or just marvel at its beauty and historic significance.

Deep Hollow Ranch

At Deep Hollow Ranch (*below*, circa 1935), Teddy Roosevelt (*below left*, circa 1900) and his Rough Riders used one of the three houses on the property after returning from the Spanish–American War in 1898. Today, Deep Hollow is still a working cattle ranch, offering trail rides and catered events.

Montauk Manor

Developer Carl Fisher built Montauk Manor in 1927. His vision was to create "the most fabulous summer resort in the western world." The Montauk Manor of today is now a luxury condominium complex.

The Great Hurricane of 1938 devastated most of the East End of Long Island. Westhampton homes were certainly not spared by the storm that brought with it winds of 120 miles per hour.

Native American Heritage

Montauk is known for its strong Native American heritage. Stephen Talkhouse, the famous Native American chief, is buried in the Montaukett burial field. In 1867, Talkhouse was displayed by P. T. Barnum as a sideshow attraction (the "Last King of the Montauks").

The HMS *Culloden* sank in Block Island Sound during a storm in 1781. This photo shows salvagers with one of the ship's cannons, which wasn't discovered until 1973. Today, the *Culloden* wreck rests only 150 feet off the shore in 20 feet of water, making it a popular diving spot.

The rich, powerful, and famous are drawn to the Hampton glitz, incredible real estate, and proximity to the beach and ocean. Even today, the Hamptons remain a summer retreat for those who can afford a seasonal residence.

THE HAMPTONS

It's difficult to pinpoint exactly when the Hamptons became *the* summer place for the rich and famous. The advent of train service during the late 19th century is one possible catalyst; the automobile in the early 20th century is another. Both allowed the wealthy of New York City to travel east to the land of beaches and ocean breezes.

Beyond its current splendor, the Hamptons—which is generally the name given to the area that encompasses Southampton, East Hampton, and Bridgehampton—has a rich history that dates back nearly four centuries. Founded by Puritans in 1640, Southampton is considered one of the oldest English settlements in New York.

Bridgehampton remains the smallest and quietest of the Hamptons. Founded around the same time as its sister communities, Bridgehampton's name was inspired by the Sagg Bridge, which was built in 1686. Today, Bridgehampton is best known for hosting the Hampton Classic Horse Show, which draws more than 40,000 spectators and 1,500 horses to the region each summer.

While living in the Hamptons is reserved for moguls and celebrities who can afford to commute by helicopter, many "regular" Long Islanders also enjoy the area each summer. Southampton's Coopers Beach is consistently rated one of the finest in the world; Main Street shopping in all the Hamptons features historic establishments, and the region's restaurants are home to some of the finest chefs in the country. Not only that, but the people watching is second to none.

Pelletreau Silver Shop

Patriot, Revolutionary War hero, and silversmith Elias Pelletreau opened his Silver Shop in Southampton in 1796. Today, the refurbished building is one of the area's oldest structures. The site is open to the public and offers educational programs.

HILDRETH'S DEPARTMENT STORE

WHEN IT COMES TO opening a business, most entrepreneurs aspire to the standard model of 25 years of growth, 25 of stability, and 25 of decline. But achieving even that is a challenging task. That's why it's safe to say that Hildreth's, which celebrated its 168th year in business in 2010, certainly broke the mold.

In the mid-19th century, Lewis Hildreth saw a need. The East End was experiencing a population boom, which meant day-to-day-living supplies were more in demand. Like any person with a vision, Hildreth decided to take a gamble—in 1842, he opened his first general store in Southampton.

By the turn of the 20th century, Southampton had grown into an enclave for affluent New Yorkers, and Hildreth's grew with it. Only Lewis wasn't around to experience this surge; he died of smallpox in 1870. The store was taken over by his wife, Amanda, and their two sons, Edgar and Henry.

Hildreth's currently operates out of four locations and is America's oldest department store. Ownership is in the hands of the 13th generation of the Hildreth family.

Clinton Academy

East Hampton's Clinton Academy was built in 1784 (shown here circa 1933) and was one of the first to be chartered by the Board of Regents. The school was coeducational from the start, preparing boys for college or careers in seafaring or surveying, while girls learned the finer points of being a lady. Today, the academy is a museum.

East Hampton

For hundreds of years, local residents have been drawn to the peaceful splendor of Main Beach in East Hampton. Its beachfront real estate remains some of the most sought after on Long Island.

The styles may have been different in 1979, but Main Street in East Hampton remains a popular place to shop and dine.

THE BOUVIERS' LEGACY

THE AFFLUENT BOUVIERS of East Hampton have spawned a legacy ingrained in American history. One of the family's two daughters,

Caroline and Jacqueline Bouvier

Jacqueline Bouvier, was born at Southampton Hospital in 1929—she'd go on to marry John F. Kennedy and become first lady. Jackie's younger sister, Caroline Lee Radziwill, owned an East Hampton family property until 2002. The girls' father, John, and many other relatives are buried in the family cemetery plot at Most Holy Trinity Catholic Cemetery on Cedar Street.

Bridgehampton

The Hamptons Classic Horse Show, held each summer in Bridgehampton, is one of the largest in the country. Shown above is Candice King riding Camillo on their way to winning the 2004 Adequan Grand Prix. The show pays proper homage to Long Island's equestrian history. The sculpture at left can be found on the show's grounds.

SHINNECOCK

The Shinnecock Indian Nation has a history on Long Island that predates both the Dutch and the English. They were whalers and fishermen long before the advent of larger boating ships; their "wampum"—shell beads tied to thread—was highly valued for trade and currency. In December 1876, 28 Shinnecock men perished attempting to save a ship stranded off East Hampton. Their heroic efforts are considered legendary.

Today, about 600 Shinnecocks reside at the 750-acre Southampton reservation. The Shinnecock's annual fall powwow celebrating the tribe's past draws thousands of visitors.

Just east of the reservation is the Shinnecock Golf Club. This elite, private club has a long tradition of employing Shinnecock Indians and is considered by many to be the oldest golf club in the United States.

Across from the golf club is Stony Brook-Southampton University. The campus centerpiece is the Shinnecock Windmill, which was originally constructed in the early 1700s and moved to its current location a century later. In its previous incarnations, the windmill served as a guesthouse for playwright Tennessee Williams during the 1950s. According to lore, Williams wrote some of his plays there.

After falling into disrepair, the windmill underwent a $250,000 refurbishment. Today it serves as a meeting place for students.

Shinnecock Tribe

This photo, taken in 1884, was titled "The Last of the Shinnecock Indians." Fortunately, the Shinnecocks and their traditions have lived on in Long Island.

Today, about 600 Shinnecock Indians reside on their 750-acre reservation in Southampton. The tribe still honors their history through artwork and the annual powwow that draws visitors from throughout the region.

Shinnecock Golf Club

Renowned architect Stanford White designed the Shinnecock Golf Club clubhouse in 1892. The first U.S. Open Golf Championship was contested at Shinnecock three years later (and won by James Foulis). The Open has been held at Shinnecock three other times; the most recent was in 2004 when South Africa's Retief Goosen (*right*) took home the title.

Main Street in Sag Harbor remains one of the South Fork's prettiest downtown shopping districts. Over the years, the road has retained its basic look, as illustrated in the photo below (taken circa 1900).

SAG HARBOR

During the American Revolution, Sag Harbor was a key British stronghold. After the war, the village remained a thriving whaling port—the third largest on the East Coast—until the 1850s. Today, the Sag Harbor Whaling Museum is a testament to the community's past; the Old Whalers Church also remains, albeit without its steeple, which was torn off during the Great Hurricane of 1938.

The end of whaling brought economic hardship to the area, though that quickly changed with the establishment of the Fahys watchcase factory in 1870. A hat factory, alongside sugar, cotton, and flour mills soon followed, and Sag Harbor drew many workers from across the region to its newly established industrial center. Later industries included the Bulova watch-case factory, E. W. Bliss Torpedo Company, Agwam Aircraft Products, and Grumman Aerospace. Bulova was the last of these industries to close (in 1981); the village now relies on the tourist trade.

Artists have long called Sag Harbor home, utilizing its coastal setting and quaint village life for inspiration. Author John Steinbeck lived there from 1955 until his death in 1968; noted poet George Sterling was born in the village. Today, the Bay Street Theatre provides summer stock productions that draw many well-known actors. Alan Alda, Julie Andrews, Alec Baldwin, and Mercedes Ruehl have all recently performed at the historic theater.

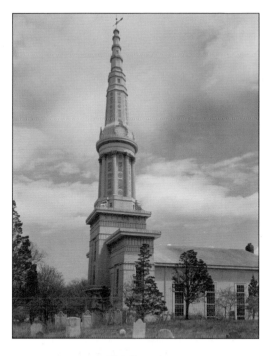

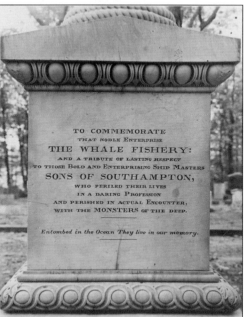

Whaling Museum

Sag Harbor's residents continue to pay their respects to the whalers of the past at locations such as the Old Whaler's Church (*above right*), the memorial to whale-ship captains (*below right*), and the Whaling Museum (*above*). Many of the region's early residents were whalers.

HAMPTON BAYS

Hampton Bays was settled in 1740 and was originally named "Good Ground." It got its new name in 1922 when residents of 11 surrounding hamlets sought to take advantage of the prestige the "Hamptons" moniker brought.

The community—which is nestled in a small coastal pocket of land between the Atlantic Ocean, Shinnecock Bay, and Peconic Bay—has grown to encompass more than 12,000 residents. Over the years, it has earned a reputation for its affordable real estate.

The area's first industry was timbering; residents, prospectors, and woodsmen razed the area's trees for timber to build homes. A sawmill powered by large sails was built in the community to cut logs into usable lumber. However, this extensive deforestation, along with fires created by railroad development in 1869, resulted in an almost treeless area by the late 1800s.

Hampton Bays is now a popular excursion point for day-trippers and for second-home purchasers who want the Hampton location without the price tag of Southampton or East Hampton. Sport fishers also flock to the local waters to fish for snapper, tuna, mahimahi, and 1,000-pound blue marlin.

In an attempt to draw attention to his farm, Martin Mauer built the "Big Duck." The 20-foot-tall, 30-foot-long duck is constructed of concrete and wood; it moved around a lot over the years before settling in Flanders. It's owned by Suffolk County and is utilized as a tourist station.

CANOE PLACE INN

CANOE PLACE WAS ONE OF the area's most popular destinations in the 18th century. In 1750, Jeremiah Culver built an inn and tavern there, which was then the only refuge for travelers between Southampton and Riverhead.

A century later, Canoe Place had grown to a community of 28 homes, a church, a tavern, and a store. Its inhabitants were almost all fishers. The Canoe Place Inn remained a favorite spot with politicians and celebrities of the day (legendary boxer John L. Sullivan, the last champion of bare-knuckle boxing, trained there for his 1892 championship bout against Jim Corbett). The original inn burned down in 1921; two people died in the blaze. However, it was later rebuilt and remains a popular dance and music club.

Shinnecock Canal

The 4,700-foot-long Shinnecock Canal opened in 1892. Located about ten miles east of Southampton, the canal connects the Great Peconic Bay and the North Fork of Long Island with Shinnecock Bay and the Atlantic Ocean. A canal lock system, the only one on Long Island, was constructed in 1919 to ease the height disparity between the two bays. Local legend claims the Shinnecocks were the first to construct the canal in the 1600s.

RIVERHEAD

Riverhead's downtown heritage can be traced to an influx of Polish immigration in 1905. Polish Town, as it quickly became known, is a 15-square-block area settled by immigrants, many of whom were farmers drawn to Long Island's East End for its rich soil and open space.

In the early 20th century, a group of Riverhead immigrants created a Polish fraternity called The Polish Roman Catholic Society of Fraternal Assistance under the Patronage of Saint Isidore, the Patron of Farmers. They built St. Isidore's Church, which opened in 1906 and is the oldest Polish Roman Catholic Church on Long Island.

In addition to the rich Polish cultural history, there are three other destinations that draw thousands of vacationers to Riverhead each summer: the stock-car track, the water park, and the aquarium.

Riverhead Raceway opened in 1949 and is one of the oldest continually operating stock-car racetracks in the country. On any given summer Saturday night, hundreds of people will watch more than 150 cars race around the quarter-mile, high-banked oval.

Splish Splash water park is consistently voted one of the country's best by various travel publications, as well as the Travel Channel. The 96-acre park opened in 1991 and boasts more than 25 rides.

In downtown Riverhead, the Atlantis Marine World Aquarium is designed around a "lost city of Atlantis" motif. It's also home to the Riverhead Foundation for Marine Research and Preservation.

3235.   MAIN STR., RIVERHEAD, L. I.   ILL. POST CARD CO., N. Y

Riverhead is the East End's largest community with a bustling Main Street that dates back to the 1800s. In this 1905 photo, horse-drawn wagon drivers were unconcerned about the large fountain situated in middle of the road.

Riverhead has had a strong Polish influence since the early 1900s when many immigrants came to the area. The community's annual Polish Festival shows off its cultural heritage.

Riverhead has many entertainment options for residents and visitors, from catching a stock-car race at Riverhead Raceway (*top*), getting up close and personal with a great white shark at Atlantis Marine World Aquarium (*above*), or taking a lazy boat ride along the Peconic River (*left*).

WINDMILLS

Looking at windmills today, it's difficult to get a sense of the role they played in history. But in colonial America, they were integral to daily life. Windmills were places to pump water, cut wood, and mill grain. Because of its flat terrain, windy conditions, and proximity to the coast, Long Island's East End—which is home to all 12 of the area's windmills—was a natural place for their construction.

In their nascency, windmills were the water coolers of their time; while villagers waited for their grain to be milled they spent time with the miller, exchanging gossip and stories about townspeople. The miller, in turn, was a central figure in his community—and not just socially. It was the miller's charge to be astute with machinery and to repair equipment used for farming and fishing.

East Hampton is home to five functioning windmills. Nathaniel Dominy V built the Old Hook Mill in 1806; it was restored to working order in 1939. The Hayground Windmill was built in 1801 and was moved in 1950 to its current location, fittingly, on Windmill Lane.

In Bridgehampton, the Beebe Windmill (circa 1820) is the only iron-geared windmill in the United States. Pantigo Mill was built on Mill Hill, and the Gardiner Windmill, constructed in 1804, offers lively historical tours.

Today, windmills are restored and operated through the generosity of historical societies and nonprofit organizations.

The Hayground Windmill

The Hayground Windmill, shown here in 1899, still has its internal machinery and unique fantail that allows it to turn into the wind.

Gardiner Windmill

The Gardiner Windmill (*left*), built in 1804, rests outside the South End Cemetery in East Hampton. Some of the tombstones date back to the 17th century.

Pantigo Windmill

The Pantigo Windmill (*left*) was built in 1804 and was moved around East Hampton several times before it found its current home next to St. Luke's Episcopalian church.

Beebe Windmill

James Beebe had the Beebe Windmill (*above*) built in 1820. It was moved around over the years before finding a home in Bridgehampton. The Beebe is the first windmill built with cast-iron gears.

Mid-Island

Where the Work Gets Done and the People Play

The Long Island Expressway (LIE) has been called "The World's Largest Parking Lot"—and for good reason. Every day, an average of 210,000 cars travel its 70.8 miles of blacktop, making it one of the country's busiest highways.

But until we come up with an alternate, *Jetsons*-like way of transportation, the LIE will remain a necessary part of life on Long Island. Without the LIE, much of Long Island would still be farmland; in fact, the central corridor—where the vast majority of Long Islanders work—developed *because* of the LIE.

Construction on the LIE started in 1939, coinciding with the opening of the Queens-Midtown Tunnel. The expressway took 33 years to complete. When the project first started, there wasn't a need for a superhighway on Long Island. Nassau and Suffolk counties were still rural areas, and only a small portion of the population needed daily access to New York City. All that changed in 1947 when William Levitt came to the region

with the dream of building a planned, affordable housing community for GIs returning home from World War II.

SUBURBIA

Levitt's plan was simple, yet unique: mass-produce affordable housing, cluster it near shopping and schools, and keep everything within commuting distance to New York City. His dream became Levittown, an area of 17,000 brand-new homes. Most developers consider Levittown to be America's first suburb.

The concept behind Levittown took off like wildfire all over Long Island, causing the population to explode from 4.6 million in 1940 to 7.1 million in 1970. Today, Levittown is one of Long Island's largest hamlets, with 55,000 residents.

The Vanderbilt Cup races were incredibly popular, exhilarating, and dangerous. Shown is the 1908 race, which was the first run on Long Island's Motor Parkway. The pit crews back then were a little different than those of today—here a racer fills up his own car with gas.

What better way to spend a sunny day than at Jumpsville USA, Long Island's trampoline park? As the long line shows, the trampolines were a popular gathering place in East Meadow in 1955.

Leroy Grumman started the Grumman Aircraft Corporation in a garage. The company grew to become Long Island's largest employer. Long Islanders built tens of thousands of planes in the Bethpage plant, including this one, seen in 1940.

Soon after the suburban boom, the LIE expanded through Nassau and Suffolk counties. Subsequently, much of Long Island's business corridor evolved in the highway's shadow—sometimes literally. Long Island's two major industrial parks in Hauppauge and Melville both abut expressway service roads.

HIP

Construction on the Hauppauge Industrial Park (HIP) began in 1964. Back then, the 1,000-acre parcel was "an antenna farm, full of monster antennas used for ship-to-shore and overseas communication before and after World War II," recalls Jack Kulka, an early developer whose firm, Kulka Contracting, is still based there.

Over the past four decades, the HIP has grown to accommodate 1,300 companies and 55,000 workers; it is the second-largest industrial park in the country, behind only California's Silicon Valley.

LAND OF DREAMS

There was a time when all of America was held rapt by space exploration, shuttle launches, and walks on the moon. Long Island was at the heart of this innovative period. In Bethpage, Grumman engineers were the first to conceptualize and then create the lunar module that landed astronauts on the moon.

Additionally, Nassau County's central corridor was where Charles Lindbergh took off in the *Spirit of St. Louis* for the first transatlantic flight. After the aviation industry moved from the area, it was developed into Roosevelt Field Shopping Center. The spot where Lindbergh took off is marked with a monument on the mall's premises.

SPORTING GOODS

In 2002 and 2009, Bethpage State Park's famous Black Course hosted the U.S. Open, making it the first public course to host golf's national championship. In 2002, record crowds of more than 200,000 people attended to witness Tiger Woods win the crown. In addition to hosting the U.S. Open, the central corridor is also the home of the Belmont Stakes, an annual horserace at Belmont Park. Today, the Belmont Stakes is the third leg of the Triple Crown.

The Long Island Ducks were a hockey team that embodied the old adage that "it's better to be really violent than good." Or something like that. The Ducks' games were so physical they inspired one of sports' most beloved cult films of all time: *Slap Shot*. Paul New-

man's character was based on John Brophy, the Ducks' rough-and-tumble player/coach. The Eastern Hockey League has since folded but the spirit of the Ducks refuses to go away—today, the Ducks are a minor-league baseball team.

Motor racing was also an allure to wealthy danger seekers on Long Island in the early 1900s when William K. Vanderbilt Jr. initiated the Vanderbilt Cup races in 1904. The races were soon moved to the newly constructed Motor Parkway, which many believe was the country's first superhighway. The 1908 Vanderbilt Cup race drew more than 250,000 fans. A section of today's Motor Parkway stretching from Hauppauge through Dix Hills is still in use by regular motorists.

The most historic mid-island spot is the Old Bethpage Village Restoration. Volunteers and workers regularly dress in period garb to show visitors what life was like in the mid-1800s. The restoration opened in 1970 and now features 51 different structures. Reenactments of old-time baseball games and Civil War battles draw more than 35,000 school children and hundreds of thousands of tourists to the site each year.

While not as eye-appealing or lavish as its coastal cousins, Long Island's central corridor plays host to many of the region's best known and best attended events. It also remains a place of rich history where the majority of today's Long Islanders live.

The Hewlett House was a private residence built in 1840. It is now part of the Old Bethpage Village Restoration property and is a shining example of what life was like on Long Island in the early 19th century.

HAUPPAUGE INDUSTRIAL PARK

In the early 1960s, a 1,000-acre tract of land in Hauppauge stood nearly vacant (an International Telephone and Telegraph antenna farm occupied a small portion of the land). Led by Lee Koppelman—a former Hauppauge civic leader and one of Long Island's most influential planners—and several forward-thinking developers, the concept of an industrial park was born. The idea was to cluster like-size companies together and surround them with housing and local transportation networks.

While Hauppauge was a real estate haven, the industrial park didn't come together overnight; initially, it lacked a road network and housing. Enter Smithtown Supervisor John V. N. Klein, who was influential in getting the industrial park up and running. Klein understood that the farther east people moved on Long Island, the more necessary local jobs became. Once the Long Island Expressway was constructed in 1965, the last piece of the puzzle was in place.

Several different developers purchased large tracts of land and started to build light industrial and warehouse buildings. Once this process began, the Hauppauge community quickly boomed. Cheap land and low taxes lured company owners.

Today, the Hauppauge Industrial Park has grown to become the largest business community of its kind east of the Mississippi River and the second largest in the entire country, behind Silicon Valley. There are currently 1,300 companies and 55,000 total employees.

Hauppauge residents enjoy the breaks they receive on their school taxes, as well as a very good school district (the businesses pick up a portion of the bill). The park also provides diversified jobs in manufacturing, engineering, and technology.

The land where these towers once stood (shown in 1940) now holds the Hauppauge Industrial Park, which is the nation's second-largest industrial park.

Long Island's second-largest employment center is Melville, a hamlet of 14,000 people. The Huntington Quadrangle is a large office complex that was constructed in 1971, renovated in 1999, and remains as a centerpiece of the region's central business corridor.

Throughout the years, Fairchild employees built thousands of planes in its Farmingdale factory. The photos at right show a still-growing company in 1934, just three years after its founding.

Newsday, Long Island's only daily newspaper, was founded in 1940 by Alicia Patterson. Its Melville printing press still churns out hundreds of thousands of newspapers each day.

PLANES, TRAINS, AND AUTOMOBILES

Because it is an island, Long Island has a unique set of transportation challenges. While the majority of the population works in Manhattan, the road and rail networks carry hundreds of thousands of commuters to an assortment of destinations each day.

Like most Americans, Long Islanders love their cars. But with the car comes a price: traffic, especially on the Long Island Expressway. The road's construction started at the base of the Midtown Tunnel in 1939 and it took nearly 33 years to complete (the last bit of asphalt was laid in Riverhead in 1972); it's more than 70 miles long and carries 210,000 cars each day.

The Long Island Rail Road (LIRR) was originally chartered in 1834 to provide train service between New York and Boston. The trip was far from easy. Travelers headed east to Greenport, then ferried across the Long Island Sound to Connecticut, *then* traveled north via train to Boston. By the mid-1850s, LIRR management refocused its attention on Long Island and acquired many of its railroads, thus expanding its service.

As for air travel, Long Island has several small commuter airports and one regional airport, Long Island MacArthur Airport. MacArthur opened in 1942 with three runways constructed by the Civil Aeronautics Administration. Lockheed Aircraft built the first hangar in 1944, and the Town of Islip, the current operator, built a terminal in 1949. The first commercial airline at MacArthur was Allegheny, which offered flights to Boston, Washington, and Philadelphia.

Through the years, MacArthur has continued to expand. Today, the airport offers four runways and two helipads at its 1,300-acre site, which reports 175,000 travelers annually.

The Long Island Expressway was completed in 1972 and carries 210,000 vehicles each day. This 1960s photo clearly illustrates the meaning behind the roadway's well-deserved nickname: "The World's Largest Parking Lot."

The LIRR

Throughout its early history, the LIRR regularly lost money. In 1900, the Pennsylvania Railroad purchased a controlling interest and infused needed capital into the railroad, which soon provided direct access to Manhattan. From that point on, the LIRR continued to expand and modernize through the early 20th century. When dwindling profits caused the railroad to go into receivership in 1949, the state of New York jumped in and began to subsidize the LIRR. Today, the Long Island Rail Road is the busiest commuter railway in the world, serving 81 million customers a year. It's also the oldest railroad to still keep its original name and charter.

Long Island's regional airport was opened in 1942 at its current Ronkonkoma site. Currently, the airport contains four runways and two helipads.

Levitt's grand vision was not just about building homes, but about building a family community. Streets were curved to avoid speeding; there were community swimming pools, village greens with shopping centers, schools, and ball fields. All were built with a family's needs in mind.

LEVITTOWN

In 1947, a new way of American life was created on Long Island when William Levitt's grand vision of planned development, built on 6,000 acres of former potato fields along the Hempstead Plains, opened as Levittown.

Levitt's timing at the end of World War II was perfect. His suburban development attracted returning GIs and their young families, police officers, lawyers, accountants, and others who wanted an affordable and safe alternative to city life. The average age of Levittown residents was just 24.

Levitt also became renowned for innovating a unique home construction model that sped up the building process. He created a standardized system of 27 steps he learned by watching military construction during a stint in the U.S. Navy.

Levitt's teams were able to churn out 30 homes a day by building on a concrete slab instead of a basement.

The completed homes were 800 square feet, consisting of four-and-a-half rooms. Levitt added landscaping and made deals with manufacturers to supply kitchen appliances, washers, blinds, radiant heat, and brick fireplaces. Total monthly charges for new homeowners rivaled or were better than those for a small apartment in Brooklyn. The price of the first Levitt homes was $7,990.

Levittown remains a vital and bustling area of Long Island, even though home prices now reach $400,000, and taxes have gone through the roof. Nonetheless, more than 53,000 Long Islanders call Levittown home, making it one of the region's largest hamlets.

At left, new residents move into some of the first Levitt homes, built in 1947. Back then, the basic model sold for $7,990. Today's Levittown, seen above, has evolved yet still provides a model example of suburbia.

Long Island visionary Robert Moses addresses guests outside the new clubhouse at Bethpage State Park during its 1933 dedication ceremony.

BETHPAGE STATE PARK

The Long Island State Park Commission opened Bethpage State Park in 1932. The 1,476-acre park is best known for its five golf courses, the first of which was constructed in 1923.

Of the five golf courses at Bethpage State Park, the Black Course is the most famous. The course was designed by renowned golf-course architect A. W. Tillinghast in the 1930s and is ranked by *Golf Digest* as the sixth most difficult course in the country. In 2002, and again in 2009, the Black Course hosted the U.S. Open. Tiger Woods captured the title in '02; Lucas Glover won it '09. The U.S. Open brought approximately 50,000 spectators to Bethpage each day and reportedly injected more than $10 million into the surrounding communities.

While internationally recognized for those two championships, Bethpage's five golf courses—Black, Blue, Green, Red, and Yellow—are known by Long Islanders as the best public golfing facility around. It's tradition for golfers to line up their cars outside the park on Friday nights in order to secure a prime spot for a Saturday morning round. And, even though it is the most difficult course to get on, golfers can still play the Black, just like Tiger Woods.

In addition to world-renowned golf, Bethpage is home to other sporting activities. The park's polo fields hosted the 1994 U.S. Open Polo Championship, and polo matches are held each Sunday through the spring and summer months. Cross-country skiing, hiking, and biking trails are also popular with local residents.

Today, Bethpage State Park is home to five public golf courses. The Black Course has played host to the U.S. Open twice. In 2002, Tiger Woods defeated Phil Mickelson, and in 2009, American Lucas Glover (*left*) took home the coveted prize. Shown above is the Black's 18th fairway with its current clubhouse in the background.

USGA

U.S. OPEN

20 09

BETHPAGE BLACK

JUNE 15-21

MOTOR PARKWAY

Long Island's Motor Parkway, which opened in 1908, was the first road built specifically for automobile use. The road was the brainchild of wealthy philanthropist William K. Vanderbilt, whose real passion was auto racing. His Vanderbilt Cup races began in 1904 and quickly became both popular and dangerous. Because the races were held on existing public roads, several accidents occurred in the early years, and a spectator was killed during a 1906 race.

Vanderbilt realized that the huge race crowds were put in peril by the fast-moving cars, so he initiated plans to build a road that was safe, police-free, and could host his race every year. The Motor Parkway's construction began in June 1908, after Vanderbilt and his investors spent more than a year obtaining right-of-way for the track. Nine miles were opened for the 1908 race, and the parkway was soon expanded to include overpasses, banked turns, a concrete tarmac, and guardrails.

The parkway was originally designed to run for 70 miles, but its final length came in at 44 miles and ran from Queens to Suffolk County. The price tag was a hefty $6 million. Soon after the Motor Parkway opened, the same problems that plagued the early Vanderbilt Cup races happened again: Four people were killed during races, causing New York to ban all road racing.

Today, sections of the Motor Parkway are still utilized in Western Suffolk County, but major portions of the road in both Nassau and Queens were either built over or have fallen into disrepair.

William K. Vanderbilt was an incredibly wealthy philanthropist, but his real passion was motor racing. His Vanderbilt Cup drew tens of thousands of racing fans to Long Island each year. When the race got too dangerous, Vanderbilt built the Motor Parkway to host the event.

American Harry Grant (seen here in his number 18 Alco Machine) won the Vanderbilt Cup race in both 1909 and 1910.

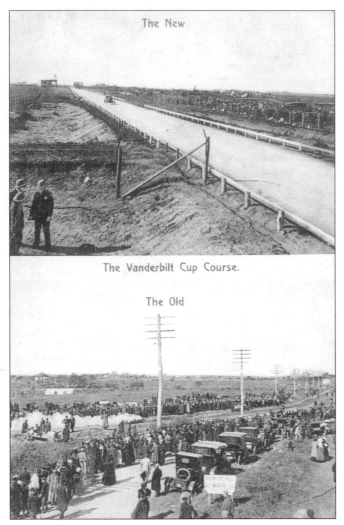

The New.

The Vanderbilt Cup Course.

The Old

Today, few people who travel on Motor Parkway have any idea of its incredible racing history.

The End of the Road

While still utilized as a toll road, innovations in paving during the 1920s (coupled with the construction of bigger and better roads that were free to use) led to the demise of the Motor Parkway. By 1938, the road was mired in back taxes and was eventually taken over by the state of New York. At right, an early Vanderbilt racer speeds around a crowd of onlookers.

THE BELMONT

In horseracing, you can't be a champion unless you win at Belmont Park. Since the track's opening in 1905, it has been the summit of equestrian competition—each of the 11 Triple Crown winners has trod upon Belmont's track. As the third—and most grueling—leg of the Triple Crown, Belmont has the distinction of making a horse's legacy.

Every year, more than 100,000 people flock to the world-renowned Belmont Stakes, hoping to witness the rare spectacle of a Triple Crown winner. The last time it happened was in 1978, when Affirmed narrowly defeated Alydar; Secretariat, who won the Belmont Stakes by 31 lengths (a track record), is undoubtedly the most famous Triple Crown champion.

The Belmont Stakes was named after sportsman, horse breeder, and financier August Belmont Sr., who helped fund the race. His son, August Jr., and a group of other investors were instrumental in the construction of the current Belmont Park.

Today, Belmont Park features daily horseracing throughout the spring, summer, and fall seasons. The Belmont Festival is held in the weeks preceding the Belmont Stakes, drawing visitors, race fans, and tourists to the surrounding Long Island communities.

Belmont Park Grandstand

The Belmont Stakes' history dates back to 1867 when the event was first held at Jerome Park in the Bronx. The track's original grandstand stood from 1905 until it was demolished in 1963; in the intermediate period, the race moved to nearby Aqueduct Park in Queens until the current and much larger grandstand opened in 1968.

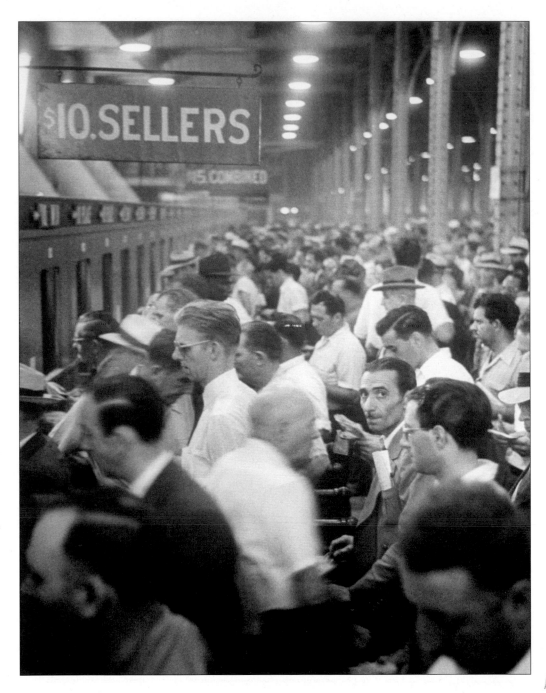

Placing bets at Belmont Park is as old as the park itself. A busy weekend of racing would easily draw tens of thousands of spectators hoping for that big win.

A 1977 horse-swapping scandal at Belmont brought unwanted national publicity to the facility, its trainers, and veterinarians.

The nine-horse field for the 136th running of the Belmont Stakes in 2004 breaks from the gate. Number four, Birdstone, was the race's victor.

Secretariat

Arguably the greatest racehorse of all time, Secretariat's 31-length victory in the 1973 Belmont Stakes was the crowning achievement of his Triple Crown performance.

Man o' War

Man o' War, who some believe is the greatest racehorse in history, made his racing debut at Belmont Park in 1919 and won the Stakes that very year. He repeated the feat in 1920 in record time, winning by 20 lengths.

SPORTS

When the Long Island Ducks entered the Eastern Hockey League (EHL) in 1959, they brought a blast of Technicolor to a fairly monochrome organization. Their brand of hard-nosed hockey was violent, destructive, and, most of all, entertaining; the Ducks quickly became one of the region's most unique and popular attractions.

Led by defenseman/head coach John Brophy, the Ducks dubbed their pugilistic approach to the game as "old-time hockey." It wasn't uncommon for more fights to break out during a game than goals scored.

Brophy—who holds the record as the EHL's career leader in penalty minutes—became the model for Reg Dunlop, the character Paul Newman played in the cult-classic movie *Slap Shot*. With his scarred face and oft-broken nose, Brophy was a polarizing figure. He was traded from the Ducks but was brought back on six different occasions; as much as he frustrated the league and the Ducks' ownership, he always attracted a crowd.

The Ducks' home, the Long Island Arena, added to the culture of the team. For years, the 4,000-seat arena used chicken wire for boards rather than Plexiglas; it was so cold that fans once built a bonfire to stay warm, and the visitor's locker room was located within a few feet of the arena's front door, causing many skirmishes between fans and players.

The creation of the New York Islanders in 1972, coupled with ongoing financial problems, caused the EHL to cease operations in 1973. It wasn't until 1999 that the Long Island Ducks reappeared, this time as a (subdued) minor-league baseball team. The baseball Ducks call Citibank Park in Central Islip home; with its 6,000 seats, 20 luxury suites, and many modern amenities, it's a long way from chicken wire and bonfires.

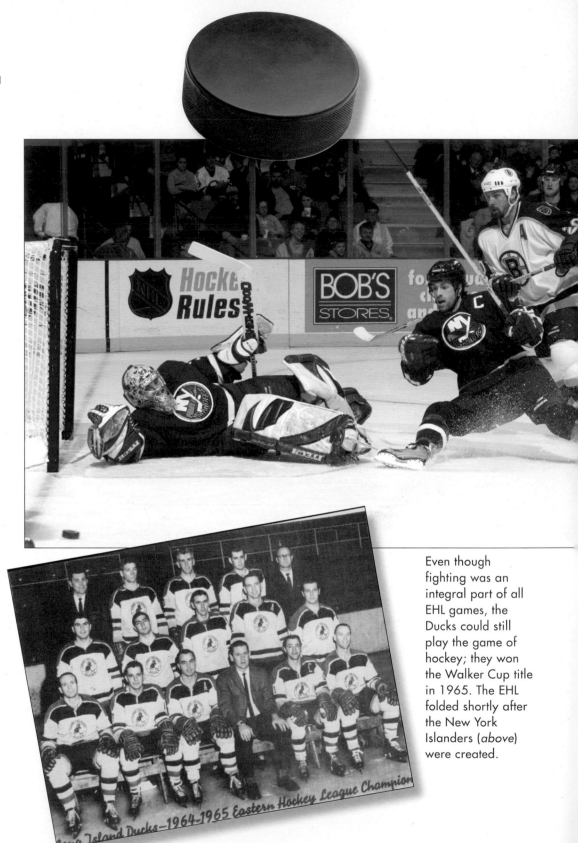

Even though fighting was an integral part of all EHL games, the Ducks could still play the game of hockey; they won the Walker Cup title in 1965. The EHL folded shortly after the New York Islanders (*above*) were created.

Long Island Ducks—1964–1965 Eastern Hockey League Champions

Ducks—Sticks to Bats

Today, the baseball Ducks have enjoyed a history of success and popularity. They're the proud owners of the Independent League attendance record, drawing more than 440,000 fans in 2001. At left, Victor Rodriguez turns a double play. In 2004, they won the Independent League Championship. Seen below is their home turf, Citibank Park.

ROOSEVELT FIELD

Today, a mall occupies the 2.26 million square feet that comprise Roosevelt Field. Nearly a century ago, Roosevelt Field was a popular airfield where legendary pilots such as Amelia Earhart and Charles Lindbergh ushered in the dawn of aviation.

One of the most famous journeys in aviation history began at Roosevelt Field; in 1927, Charles Lindbergh's *Spirit of St. Louis* took off for the first transatlantic flight from the Nassau airstrip. A monument outside the mall marks Lindbergh's takeoff spot.

The airstrip closed in 1951, soon after the birth of Levittown and the beginning of the suburban boom on Long Island. Developer William Zeckendorf purchased the open property and was determined to construct a shopping center. In 1955, ground was broken at Roosevelt Field for the $35-million, open-air shopping center. The mall officially opened in 1956; its original and largest anchor store was a 340,000-square-foot Macy's.

Roosevelt Field's location—in the middle of Nassau County and only 25 miles from Manhattan—made it a popular destination for locals and tourists. Nearby Roosevelt Raceway was a landmark in harness racing until it closed in 1988.

As for the mall, it has undergone numerous expansions and refurbishments, including its enclosure in 1963. It has grown to become the largest mall in New York and the fifth largest in the country. While Macy's remains as a relic from the mall's golden years, many different retailers have come and gone. But one thing that does stay the same is the mall's tremendous popularity: Roosevelt Field averages more than 2.5 million visits a month, and ten different bus lines bring in 17,000 people a day.

Trotting horse Jasmin gets a friendly peck from his jockey after winning an international harness race at Roosevelt Raceway in Westbury in 1959. Harness Racing at Roosevelt was hugely popular on Long Island in the mid-20th century. The half-mile track closed in 1988.

Roosevelt Field Mall

Roosevelt Field is the fifth-largest indoor mall in the country. Charles Lindbergh's famous 1927 transatlantic flight originated on this site. A stone monument (*below*) marks Lindy's takeoff spot.

FLIGHT

There's something awe-inspiring about looking up at an endless blue sky and imagining the possibilities. From 1918 to 1939, during The Golden Age of Aviation, a number of these dreamers stopped looking at the Long Island sky and imagining; instead, they started *doing*.

In 1909, Glenn Curtiss brought his biplane, *The Golden Flyer,* to Nassau's Hempstead Plains to utilize the area's three airstrips and join other aviation innovators. Two years later, the first transcontinental flight originated on Long Island when Cal Rodgers took 49 days to reach California in a Wright biplane.

The pioneering work completed in the following years led to safety innovations and developments that transformed flying from a dangerous sport to a viable means of transportation. In 1937, the first regular transatlantic flights began when Pan American Martin ferried passengers from Manhasset Bay in their "flying boats" to Europe.

Because Long Island was home to many of flight's early engineers and pilots, it became a hub for military aircraft construction during World War II. While many companies were involved in airplane construction on Long Island, Grumman and Republic dominated the local industry, employing more than 100,000 people.

After the war, Grumman expanded its reach—to say the least—when its engineers built the first lunar module. Today, Grumman still employs several thousand Long Islanders. Currently, more than 200 Long Island companies engineer and produce parts for some of the world's best-known aircraft.

Glenn H. Curtiss

Glenn H. Curtiss (*right*) was a pioneering aviator who first came to Long Island's Hempstead Plains in 1909 to test and innovate the aircraft of the time. The photo above shows Curtiss's 1914 test flight of a restored Aerodrome created by Samuel Pierpont Langley, another flight pioneer.

Mitchel Field

With the exception of Kitty Hawk, North Carolina, Long Island is probably the most influential region in the world related to the advent, growth, and engineering of flight. Mitchel Field (*below*) also housed a military training base. Shown at left are young soldiers taking target practice in 1942.

Side view of the three motored Caproni entered in

Roosevelt Field

Roosevelt Field was at the forefront of The Golden Age of Aviation in the United States. Located in the Hempstead Plains—a flat area with incredible sight lines—pioneering aviators came from around the world to fly and test their machines. At right is Charles Lindbergh, shown in 1923.

Female aviators were also regular visitors to Roosevelt Field. Celebrated flyer Amelia Earhart is shown here at Roosevelt Field in 1936, only months before she disappeared while attempting to circumnavigate the globe in 1937.

The Cradle of Aviation Museum in Garden City is a testament to Long Island's place as a leader in the history of flight.

GRUMMAN

In his youth, Leroy Grumman was just a naval reserve private who couldn't get accepted to flight training (it didn't help that he was misdiagnosed for having flat feet). From an early age, the Huntington native had a passion for aviation. Though known for his shyness, there's one thing that everyone saw in Grumman—that when he looked to the sky, he saw a world of fantastic possibilities.

After a clerical error allowed Grumman to enroll in a pilot trainee course at the Massachusetts Institute of Technology, the hopeful aviator took off for the skies and never looked back.

After World War I, Grumman and his longtime friend and colleague, Leon Swirbul, raised $32,000 to fund their own company. Grumman Aeronautical Engineering opened its doors on January 2, 1930.

Initially, the company stayed afloat by, well, building floats. Aluminum floats, to be exact. It wasn't until 1932 that Grumman would give his company the break it needed. After hounding the U.S. Navy for contracts, Grumman finally reeled in a major deal with his patent for retractable landing gear. From then on, the sailing was smooth (as were the landings).

Grumman Aeronautical went on to form a lasting relationship with the navy; throughout World War II, the company developed an assortment of fighter planes. In fact, those fighter planes dominated World War II—Grumman Hellcats have the highest kill ratio in aircraft history.

Like any innovator, Grumman had the ability to adapt to the times. In 1962, NASA contracted Grumman to construct its lunar module. The company built a total of 13 moon ships.

Despite the passing of its original founders, Grumman remained independently held until 1994 when the Northrop Corporation bought the company. Headquarters are still located in Bethpage.

Long Islanders working for Grumman in Bethpage helped engineer and build the lunar module that allowed the crew of *Apollo 11* to land safely on and return from the moon. The lunar module is considered one of the world's greatest engineering feats and remains a source of pride for all Long Islanders.

Today, Grumman has merged with Northrop and has a smaller presence on Long Island. The company's spirit of innovation and exploration are memorialized on the above mural, which is shown at its current Long Island facility.

OLD BETHPAGE VILLAGE

While vestiges of Long Island's rich history still exist across the entire region, few places allow visitors to actually experience days gone by like the Old Bethpage Village Restoration.

The restoration, which is sometimes called a "living museum," is set on a 209-acre site in Eastern Nassau County; it consists of 51 preserved and 7 rebuilt structures. The buildings were clustered to re-create the look of a Long Island farming village, circa the mid-1800s.

Old Bethpage Village opened in 1970 on its current site, which only housed the Powell Farmhouse at that time. Plainview's Manetto Hill Methodist Church was the first structure moved to the site. Since then, Nassau County officials and workers had other buildings moved from other places, saving many from almost certain demolition. Popular structures in the village include Layton's candy store, the Bach Blacksmith Shop, and the Noon Inn (a working tavern).

Today, in addition to drawing thousands of visitors, the campus hosts more than 35,000 local schoolchildren for educational field trips. They are shown how children of that era were taught in a one-room schoolhouse and are able to participate in demonstrations of farming, tending of animals, and family life.

During the summer, the restoration is host to Civil War reenactments, a lavish Fourth of July celebration, and vintage baseball games, played in period garb utilizing mid-1800s rules and equipment. Each fall the village restoration is also the site of the annual Long Island Fair.

A slice of Americana runs rampant through the Old Bethpage Village Farmhouse, where visitors are treated to a bygone era through farming exhibitions and old-time baseball reenactments. The Powell House (*right*) is the only original building on the site. It has been restored to its original 1855 condition.

Getting a turkey from Zorn's has been a Long Island tradition since 1940.

ZORN'S

In 1940, during the era before the suburban explosion of nearby Levittown, turkey farmer Peter Zorn took Bethpage by storm. From his own farm, Zorn began selling turkeys to local residents. The freshness of his products, convenience to his customers, and great service enabled the popularity of the Zorn Poultry Farm to explode.

As his reputation and his customer base grew, Zorn quickly increased and diversified his output, making products like butter, eggs, homemade pies, and breads.

Zorn was a man ahead of his time; he constantly tinkered with his products and methods, and eventually became known as a progenitor to take-out food. Zorn's business expanded, and he

was soon catering complete meals of poultry, potatoes, vegetables, and bread. The Zorn name became synonymous with the holidays; lines would circle around the building during Thanksgiving and Christmas. Obtaining a Zorn bird was a must.

The Zorn business continues to expand today. There are now three retail locations, the original one in Bethpage, as well as stores in Bellmore and East Meadow. One hundred and forty employees prepare and sell more than 15,000 turkeys each year, and the original Zorn recipes are still used. "We have a fanatical, loyal customer base," said Monique Zorn, director of customer relations and Peter's granddaughter. The company is currently considering franchising the Zorn brand.

HIGH-TECH HISTORY

Brookhaven National Laboratory (BNL) was established in 1947 after nine major research universities—Columbia, Cornell, Harvard, Johns Hopkins, MIT, Penn, Princeton, RIT, and Yale—banded together to establish a nuclear-science facility. The lab's original goal was to discover and utilize a peaceful use for the atom.

Under the auspices of the U.S. Department of Energy, BNL has made numerous breakthroughs in both science and health. The lab was one of the first to discover the link between salt and hypertension, and its work on radiation has proven vital to cancer treatment. Neurological studies have uncovered the roots of psychiatric disorders, drug addiction, and the effects of L-dopa on Parkinson's. To date, the lab's scientists have won six Nobel Prizes, one in chemistry and five in physics.

Life at BNL isn't all work—there's some play as well. In 1958, BNL scientist William Higinbotham developed the world's first video game, *Tennis for Two*. Other public work has included the development of the magnetically levitated train, environmentally efficient oil burners, and advanced computer-chip design.

Today, BNL's 5,265-acre campus features its own ZIP code, fire department, and police department, as well as the regional office of the National Weather Service. It has a staff of approximately 3,000 scientists, engineers, and technicians; its 4,000 annual guest researchers make it one of the region's largest and most influential employers.

The sprawling Upton campus of Brookhaven National Lab is more than 5,000 acres in size. It also happens to be a place where groundbreaking experiments are conducted daily related to energy, science, and health.

General Electric built this electrostatic accelerator for Brookhaven National Laboratory in 1949 to aid in its ongoing atomic research.

This one-and-a-half-ton lead shield is raised from the water canal at Brookhaven National Laboratory's atomic reactor in 1955. The scientist is protected from the radioactive contents by the lead and its water.

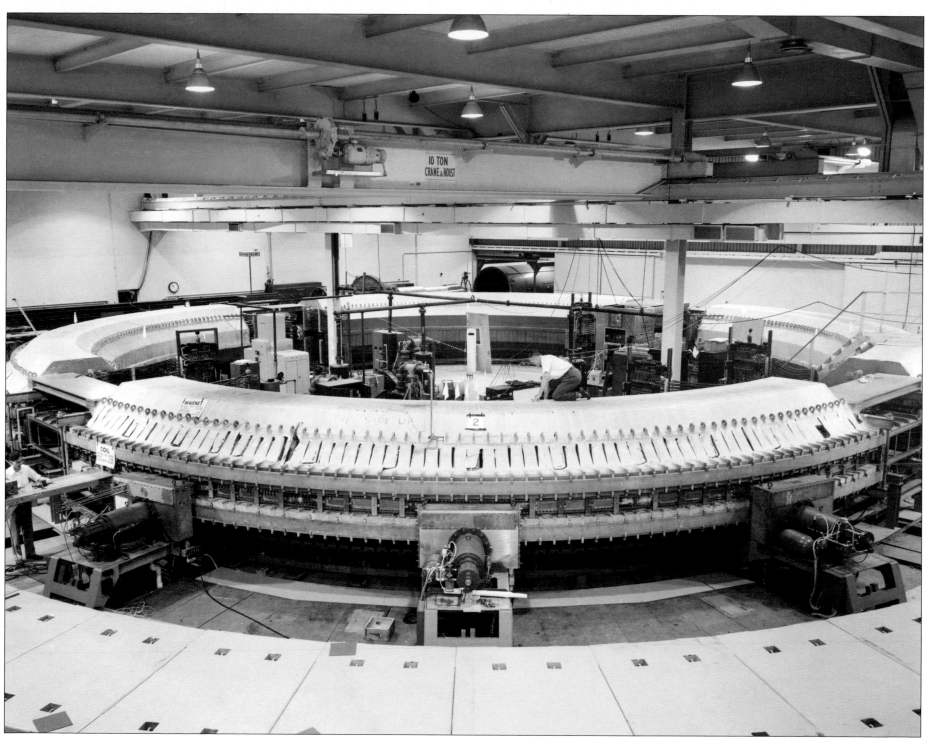

Two scientists conduct experiments working in a nuclear laboratory at Brookhaven National Laboratory.

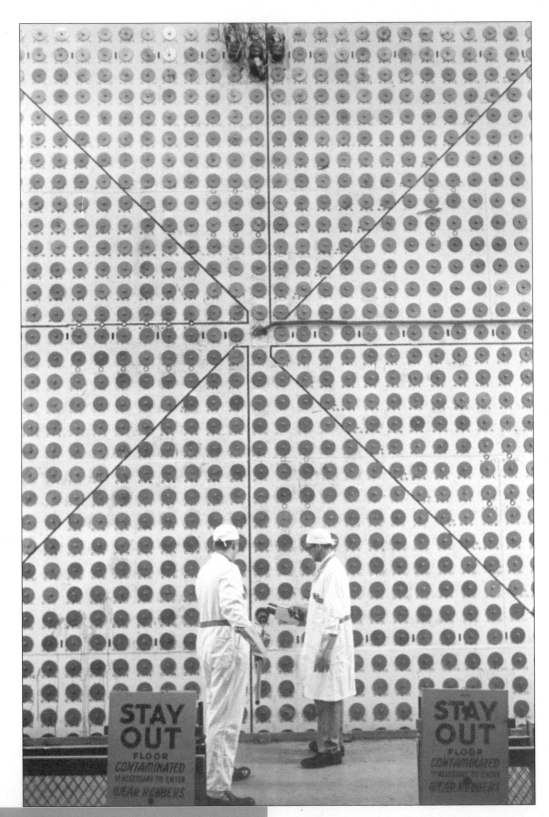

While these two scientists are loading the nuclear reactor at Brookhaven National Laboratory in 1958, the message is simple for others: STAY OUT.

BROOKHAVEN'S UNIVERSE

EVER WONDER WHAT THE UNIVERSE looked like in the moments after the Big Bang? Good, because so did the physicists at the Brookhaven National Laboratory. That's why in 2000 they dropped $600 million on the construction of a Relativistic Heavy Ion Collider (RHIC), a 2.4-mile tunnel that smashes intersecting beams of ions together at the speed of light.

Though infinitely complex in its actual functions, the purpose of the RHIC is to re-create the universe as it was 15 billion years ago. By further understanding how the physical world works, from the tiniest particles to entire solar systems, BNL physicists can continue to be on the cutting edge of technological and medical advances.

The RHIC didn't come without some controversy though. Critics feared that Brookhaven physicists were unequipped to predict what kind of catastrophes the RHIC could create. Catastrophes like space vacuums and black holes that have the potential to devastate the Earth in seconds.

Luckily, none of those things happened. In fact, the success of the RHIC has spawned the creation of a sibling, the Large Hadron Collider near Geneva, Switzerland.

The LHC, which usurped the RHIC as the world's largest collider, has also been met with resistance, including some speculation involving time travel.

Beam us up, Scotty.

Camp Upton

Before it became Brookhaven Lab, the property was part of Camp Upton (*above*), an area used to train and house soldiers beginning in 1917. After being deactivated in 1920, the camp was back in business again in 1940 to help with the training and mobilization of soldiers for World War II. One of Camp Upton's most famous residents was conductor Irving Berlin, who wrote the musical *Yip-Yip-Yaphank* there in 1918. Berlin is shown at right in 1942, leading soldiers in a rehearsal for another production, *This is the Army*.

Index